D0372547

HTML and XHTML
Pocket Reference

FOURTH EDITION

HTML and XHTML
Pocket Reference

Jennifer Niederst Robbins

O'REILLY®

Beijing · Cambridge · Farnham · Köln · Sebastopol · Taipei · Tokyo

HTML and XHTML Pocket Reference, Fourth Edition

by Jennifer Niederst Robbins

Published by O'Reilly Media, Inc., 1005 Gravenstein Highway North, Sebastopol, CA 95472.

O'Reilly books may be purchased for educational, business, or sales promotional use. Online editions are also available for most titles (*http://my.safari booksonline.com*). For more information, contact our corporate/institutional sales department: (800) 998-9938 or *corporate@oreilly.com*.

Editors: Steven Weiss and Simon St.Laurent
Production Editor: Loranah Dimant
Proofreader: Loranah Dimant
Indexer: Ellen Troutman Zaig
Cover Designer: Karen Montgomery
Interior Designer: David Futato
Illustrator: Robert Romano

Printing History:

January 2000:	First Edition.
January 2002:	Second Edition.
May 2006:	Third Edition.
December 2009:	Fourth Edition.

ISBN: 978-0-596-80586-9

[TM]

1260481522

HTML and XHTML Pocket Reference

HTML (*HyperText Markup Language*) is the markup language used to turn text documents into web pages and applications. The fundamental purpose of HTML as a markup language is to provide a *semantic* description (the meaning) of the content and establish a document *structure* (a hierarchy of elements). It is not concerned with *presentation*, such as how the document will look in a browser. Presentation is the job of Cascading Style Sheets, which is outside the scope of this book.

This pocket reference provides a concise yet thorough listing of the elements and attributes specified in the HTML 4.01 and XHTML 1.0 Recommendations as well as HTML5, which is in development as a Working Draft as of this writing. The text uses the shorthand "(X)HTML" for concepts that apply to all of these markup standards.

For updates and details on all versions, see the W3C's HTML home page at *www.w3.org/html*. HTML5 is a joint effort between the W3C and the WHATWG (Web Hypertext Application Technology Working Group). See the latest HTML5 developments at *www.whatwg.org/specs*.

This book is organized into the following sections:

- "HTML 4.01 Overview"
- "HTML5 Overview"
- "XHTML Overview"
- "Common Attributes and Events"
- "Alphabetical List of Elements"
- "Elements Organized by Function"
- "Character Entities"
- "Specifying Color"

HTML 4.01 Overview

The HTML 4.01 Recommendation (1999) is the best established and supported HTML specification as of this writing. This section covers the basic structure of HTML 4.01 documents.

Three Versions of HTML 4.01

Both the HTML 4.01 and XHTML 1.0 Recommendations encompass three slightly different specification documents, called *Document Type Definitions* (or *DTDs*). DTDs define every element, attribute, and entity along with the rules for their use. The three versions are:

Transitional DTD

> The Transitional DTD includes all deprecated elements and attributes in order to be backward compatible with the legacy behavior of most browsers. Deprecated elements and attributes are permitted but discouraged from use.

Strict DTD

> This version excludes all elements and attributes that have been *deprecated* (such as `font` and `align`) to reinforce the separation of document structure from presentation.

Frameset DTD

The Frameset DTD includes the same elements as the Transitional DTD with the addition of elements for creating framed web pages (`frameset`, `frame`, and `noframe`). The Frameset DTD is kept separate because the structure of a framed document (where `frameset` replaces `body`) is fundamentally different from regular HTML documents.

HTML 4.01 Document Structure

This markup sample shows the minimal structure of an HTML 4.01 document. This example uses the Strict HTML DTD:

```
<!DOCTYPE HTML PUBLIC "-//W3C//DTD HTML 4.01//EN"
   "http://www.w3.org/TR/html4/strict.dtd">
<html>
  <head>
    <title>Document Title</title>
  </head>
  <body>
     Content of document . . .
  </body>
</html>
```

HTML 4.01 DOCTYPE Declarations

The first line of the document structure example just shown is the *Document Type Declaration* (or *DOCTYPE declaration*) that declares the DTD version used for the document. It is used to check the document for validity. Some browsers also use the inclusion of a complete DOCTYPE declaration to switch into a standards-compliant rendering mode.

The `<!DOCTYPE>` (document type) declaration contains two methods for pointing to DTD information: one is a publicly recognized document identifier, and the other is a specific URL in case the browsing device does not recognize the public identifier. The DOCTYPE declarations for each HTML version must be used exactly as they appear here:

HTML 4.01 Strict

```
<!DOCTYPE HTML PUBLIC "-//W3C//DTD HTML 4.01//EN"
"http://www.w3.org/TR/HTML4.01/strict.dtd">
```

HTML 4.01 Transitional

```
<!DOCTYPE HTML PUBLIC "-//W3C//DTD HTML 4.01
Transitional//EN"
"http://www.w3.org/TR/HTML4.01/loose.dtd">
```

HTML 4.01 Frameset

```
<!DOCTYPE HTML PUBLIC "-//W3C//DTD HTML 4.01 Frameset//EN"
"http://www.w3.org/TR/HTML4.01/frameset.dtd">
```

HTML5 Overview

HTML5, which aims to make HTML more useful for creating web applications as well as semantically marked up documents, is not yet a formal Recommendation as of this writing, however, it is beginning to gain browser support and is already being used for web and mobile application development.

HTML5 uses HTML 4.01 and the legacy behavior of browsers as a starting point, using the *Document Object Model* (DOM, the "tree" formed by a document's structure) as its basis rather than a particular set of syntax rules. HTML5 can be written with HTML syntax (called the HTML serialization of HTML5) or according to the stricter syntax of XML (XML serialization, or "XHMTL 5") if XML parsing is required.

NOTE

Because HTML5 is still in development, the details are changing rapidly. The HTML5 elements and attributes in this book are based on the WHATWG HTML5 Working Draft dated December 9, 2009.

For the most recent version, go to *www.whatwg.org/ specs/web-apps/current-work/multipage/*. For a list of the ways HTML5 differs from HTML 4.01, see *dev.w3.org/ html5/html4-differences*.

New in HTML5

HTML5 offers new features (elements, attributes, event handlers, and APIs) for easier web application development and more sophisticated form handling. There are also new semantic elements for marking up page content. Most of the purely presentational or poorly supported elements and attributes in HTML 4.01 have been dropped from HTML5, however, a few have been redefined or reinstated.

Elements

Details for each of these elements may be found later in the section "Alphabetical List of Elements":

article	footer	rp
aside	header	rt
audio	hgroup	ruby
canvas	keygen	section
command	mark	source
datalist	meter	time
details	nav	video
embed	output	
figure	progress	

New input Types

HTML5 introduces the following new input control types (indicated as values for the type attribute for the input element): color, date, datetime, datetime-local, email, month, number, range, search, tel, time, url, week.

Attributes and Events

The Global Attributes and Events available for all elements in HTML5 are listed and described in detail in the "Common Attributes and Events" section. New HTML5 attributes are listed with their respective elements and labeled ***HTML5 only*** in the "Alphabetical List of Elements" section.

APIs

With a growing demand for interactive content on web pages, HTML5 introduces several APIs (*Application Programming Interfaces*) for standardizing the creation of web applications.

There are APIs for the following:

- Two-dimensional drawing in conjunction with the new `canvas` element
- Playing video and audio files, used with the new `video` and `audio` elements
- Offline web applications
- Registering applications for certain protocols or media types
- Editing documents, including a new global `contentedita ble` attribute
- Drag and drop functionality (including the new `dragga ble` attribute)
- Exposing the browser history and allowing pages to add to without breaking the back button
- Cross-document messaging

HTML5 Document Structure

HTML5 has only one version and does not reference a DTD, but HTML5 documents still require a simplified DOCTYPE declaration to trigger standards mode rendering in browsers. The following is the basic structure of an HTML5 document:

```
<!DOCTYPE html>
<html>
  <head>
    <title>Document Title</title>
  </head>
  <body>
      Content of document . . .
  </body>
</html>
```

HTML5 documents written in XML syntax do not require a DOCTYPE but may include an XML declaration. They should also be served as the MIME type `application/xhtml+xml` or `application/xml`. The following is a simple HTML5 document written in the XML syntax:

```
<?xml version="1.0" encoding="UTF-8"?>
<html xmlns="http://www.w3.org/1999/xhtml">
  <head>
    <title>Document Title</title>
  </head>
  <body>
      Content of document . . .
  </body>
</html>
```

HTML5 Browser Support

As of this writing, HTML5 is still in its earliest days and has only limited browser support. A few features are supported in Firefox 3.5+, Safari 3+, Chrome 2+, and Opera 9+ (Opera supports nearly all of the HTML5 Forms features). Internet Explorer supports `contentEditable`, but otherwise has not promised support for HTML5 in its version 10 release, so we'll have to stay tuned a while to see what comes after that. In the meantime, JavaScript can be used to make browsers recognize HTML5 elements.

Many developers are looking to the mobile world as the arena where HTML5 will take hold in the form of web-based applications.

The following resources are useful for tracking HTML5 real-world support and use:

- "When Can I Use..." (*a.deveria.com/caniuse/*): A comparison of browser support for HTML5, CSS3, and other web technologies maintained by Alexis Deveria.

- Wikipedia "Comparison of Layout Engines (HTML5)" (*en.wikipedia.org/wiki/Comparison_of_layout_engines_(HTML_5)*): Charts show HTML5 support by the major browser layout engines.

- *HTML5 Doctor, Helping you Implement HTML5 today* (*html5doctor.com*): Articles about HTML5 development and implementation, curated by Richard Clark, Bruce Lawson, Tom Leadbetter, Jack Osborne, Mike Robinson, and Remy Sharp.

XHTML Overview

XHTML 1.0 (eXtensible HyperText Markup Language) is a reformulation of HTML 4.01 according to the stricter syntax rules of XML (eXtensible Markup Language). In other words, the elements are the same, but there are additional restrictions for document markup as listed in the next section.

On July 2, 2009, the World Wide Web Consortium (W3C) officially discontinued the XHTML 2.0 project, focusing its resources instead on HTML5 (which can also be written in XML syntax). Although no new XHTML specifications are being developed, XHTML documents will continue to be supported by popular browsers for the foreseeable future.

How XHTML Differs from HTML

Because XHTML is an XML language, its syntax is stricter and differs from HTML in these key ways:

- All element names and attributes must be lowercase. For example, `<a href="example.com">...</a>`.
- All elements must be terminated—that is, they must include an end tag. For example, `<p>...</p>`.
- Empty elements must be terminated as well. This is done by including a slash at the end of the tag. A space is commonly added before the slash for backward compatibility with older browsers. For example, `<hr />`, `<img />`, `<meta />`.
- All attribute values must be contained in quotation marks (either single or double). For example, `<td colspan="2">`.

- All attribute values must be explicit and may not be minimized to one word, as is permitted in HTML. For example:

  — `checked="checked"`

  — `selected="selected"`

  — `multiple="multiple"`

- Nesting restrictions are more strictly enforced. These restrictions are explicitly stated:

  — An `a` element cannot contain another `a` element.

  — The `pre` element cannot contain `img`, `object`, `applet`, `big`, `small`, `sub`, `sup`, `font`, or `basefont`.

  — The `form` element may not contain other `form` elements.

  — A `button` element cannot contain `a`, `form`, `input`, `select`, `textarea`, `label`, `button`, `iframe`, or `isindex`.

  — The `label` element cannot contain other `label` elements.

- The special characters <, >, &, ', and " must always be represented by their character entities, including when they appear within attribute values. For example, `&lt;`, `&gt;`, `&amp;`, `&apos;`, and `&quot;` (respectively).

- In HTML, the `name` attribute may be used for the elements `a`, `applet`, `form`, `frame`, `iframe`, `img`, and `map`. The `name` attribute and the `id` attribute may be used in HTML to identify document fragments. XHTML documents must use `id` instead of `name` for identifying document fragments in the aforementioned elements. In fact, the `name` attribute for these elements has been deprecated in the XHTML 1.0 specification.

- XHTML documents should be served as XML applications, not as HTML text documents. More specifically, the server should be configured to serve XHTML documents with the Content-type header set to `application/xhtml+xml`. If it is not possible to configure the server, the content type may be specified in a `meta` element in the document's `head`, as shown in this example:

```
<meta http-equiv="content-type"
    content="application/xhtml+xml; charset=UTF-8" />
```

Unfortunately, some popular browsers (Internet Explorer in particular) cannot parse XHTML documents as XML, causing pages to break. For this reason, many developers serve XHTML documents as **text/html** instead, although the W3C discourages this, and it is not possible if the document includes code from other XML namespaces. For more information on XHTML MIME types, see *www.w3.org/TR/xhtml-media-types/*.

XHTML 1.0 Document Structure

Like HTML 4.01, XHTML 1.0 has three DTD versions: transitional, strict, and frameset.

This markup sample shows the minimal structure of an XHTML 1.0 document as specified in the XHTML 1.0 Recommendation. This document was written using the XHTML Transitional DTD:

```
<!DOCTYPE html PUBLIC "-//W3C//DTD XHTML 1.0 Transitional/
/EN"
  "http://www.w3.org/TR/xhtml1/DTD/xhtml1-transitional.
dtd">
<html xmlns="http://www.w3.org/1999/xhtml" xml:lang="en"
lang="en">
  <head>
    <title>Document Title</title>
  </head>
  <body>
      Content of document . . .
  </body>
</html>
```

Note that the **html** root element includes XML namespace (**xmlns**) and language (**xml:lang**) identification.

XHTML documents may optionally include an XML declaration before the DOCTYPE declaration, as shown in this example:

```
<?xml version="1.0" encoding="UTF-8"?>
<!DOCTYPE html PUBLIC "-//W3C//DTD XHTML 1.0 Strict//EN"
    "http://www.w3.org/TR/xhtml1/DTD/xhtml1-strict.dtd">
```

An XML declaration is not required when the character encoding is the UTF-8 default. Because XML declarations are problematic for even standards-compliant browsers as of this writing, they are generally omitted.

NOTE

XHTML5 documents do not require a DOCTYPE declaration.

XHTML DOCTYPE Declarations

The DOCTYPE declarations for each XHTML version must be used exactly as they appear here:

XHTML 1.0 Strict

```
<!DOCTYPE html PUBLIC "-//W3C//DTD XHTML 1.0 Strict//EN"
 "http://www.w3.org/TR/xhtml1/DTD/xhtml1-strict.dtd">
```

XHTML 1.0 Transitional

```
<!DOCTYPE html PUBLIC "-//W3C//DTD XHTML 1.0
Transitional//EN"
 "http://www.w3.org/TR/xhtml1/DTD/xhtml1-transitional.dtd">
```

XHTML 1.0 Frameset

```
<!DOCTYPE html PUBLIC "-//W3C//DTD XHTML 1.0
Frameset//EN"
 "http://www.w3.org/TR/xhtml1/DTD/xhtml1-frameset.dtd">
```

XHTML 1.1

The XHTML 1.1 Recommendation features only one DTD that is similar to Strict in that it does not include deprecated elements and attributes:

```
<!DOCTYPE html PUBLIC "-//W3C//DTD XHTML 1.1//EN"
 "http://www.w3.org/TR/xhtml11/DTD/xhtml11.dtd">
```

Common Attributes and Events

A number of attributes are shared by nearly all elements. To save space, they have been abbreviated in this reference as they are in the Recommendations. This section serves as a reference for "Alphabetical List of Elements" and explains each attribute's shorthand.

In HTML 4.01/XHTML 1.0, the attributes and events are divided into groups called *Core*, *Internationalization*, *Focus*, and *Events*. In HTML5, there is one set of *Global Attributes* that applies to all HTML elements.

HTML 4.01 and XHTML 1.0

Core

When *Core* is listed under Attributes, it refers to the set of core attributes that may be applied to the majority of elements (as noted in each element listing):

id
> Assigns a unique identifying name to the element

class
> Assigns one or more classification names to the element

style
> Associates style information with an element

title
> Provides a title or advisory information about the element

Internationalization

When *Internationalization* appears in the attribute list, it means the element accepts the set of attributes used to specify language and reading direction:

dir
> Specifies the direction of the element (left to right or right to left).

`lang`

> Specifies the language for the element by its language code.

`xml:lang`

> **XHTML only**. Specifies language for elements in XHTML documents.

Focus

Focus refers to the state of being highlighted and ready for user input, such as for a link or form element. When *Focus* is listed, it indicates that the following attributes and events related to bringing focus to the element are applicable:

`accesskey="`*`character`*`"`

> Assigns an access key (shortcut key command) to the link. Access keys are also used for form fields. The value is a single character. Users may access the element by hitting Alt-<*key*> (PC) or Ctrl-<*key*> (Mac).

`onblur`

> Occurs when an element loses focus either by the pointing device or by tabbing navigation.

`onfocus`

> Occurs when an element receives focus either by the pointing device or by tabbing navigation.

`tabindex="`*`number`*`"`

> Specifies the position of the current element in the tabbing order for the current document. The value must be between 0 and 32,767. It is used for tabbing through the links on a page (or fields in a form).

Events

When *Events* is listed for the element, it indicates that the core events used by scripting languages are applicable to the element. Additional events that are not part of the core events are listed separately for each element:

onclick
> Occurs when the pointing device button is clicked over an element

ondblclick
> Occurs when the pointing device button is double-clicked over an element

onkeydown
> Occurs when a key is pressed down over an element

onkeypress
> Occurs when a key is pressed and released over an element

onkeyup
> Occurs when a key is released over an element

onmousedown
> Occurs when the pointing device button is pressed over an element

onmousemove
> Occurs when the pointing device is moved while it is over an element

onmouseout
> Occurs when the pointing device is moved away from an element

onmouseover
> Occurs when the pointing device is moved onto an element

onmouseup
> Occurs when the pointing device button is released over an element

HTML5

Global attributes

In addition to id, class, style, title, dir, lang, accesskey, and tabindex carried over from HTML 4.01, HTML5 adds the following global attributes that are applicable to all elements:

`contenteditable="true|false"`

Indicates the user can edit the element. This attribute is already well supported in current browser versions.

`contextmenu="`*id of menu element*`"`

Specifies a context menu that applies to the element. The context menu must be requested by the user, for example, by a right-click.

`draggable="true|false"`

Indicates the element is draggable, meaning it can be moved by clicking and holding on it, then moving it to a new position in the window.

`hidden` (`hidden="hidden"` *in XHTML)*

Prevents the element and its descendants from being rendered in the user agent (browser). Any scripts or form controls in hidden sections will still execute, but they will not be presented to the user.

`itemid="`*text*`"`

Part of the microdata system for embedding machine-readable data, the `itemid` attribute indicates a globally recognized identifier (such as an ISBN for a book). It is used in conjunction with `itemtype` in the same element containing `itemscope`.

`itemprop="`*text*`"`

Part of the microdata system for embedding machine-readable data, the `itemprop` attribute provides the name of the property. The content of the element provides its value. The value may also be a URL provided by the `href` attribute in `a` elements or the `src` attribute in `img`.

`itemref="`*space-separated list of IDs*`"`

Part of the microdata system for embedding machine-readable data, the `itemref` attribute specifies a list of elements (by ID values) on the current page to be included in an *item*. The `itemref` attribute must be used in the same element as the `itemscope` attribute that established the item.

`itemscope`

Part of the microdata system for embedding machine-readable data, `itemscope` creates a new *item*, a group of properties (name/value pairs).

`itemtype="URL or reversed DNS label"`

Part of the microdata system for embedding machine-readable data, the `itemtype` attribute indicates a standardized item type indicated by a URL (e.g., *http://vocab.example.net/book*) or a reversed DNS label (e.g., com.example.person). The `itemtype` attribute is used in the same element containing the `itemscope` attribute.

`spellcheck="true|false"`

Indicates the element is to have its spelling and grammar checked.

HTML5 event handlers

Unless otherwise specified, the following event handler content attributes may be specified on any HTML element:

onabort	onmessage*
onafterprint	onmousedown
onbeforeprint	onmousemove
onbeforeunload	onmouseout
onblur*	onmouseover
oncanplay	onmouseup
oncanplaythrough	onmousewheel
onchange	onoffline
onclick	ononline
oncontextmenu	onpagehide*
ondblclick	onpageshow*
ondrag	onpopstate*
ondragend	onpause
ondragenter	onplay
ondragleave	onplaying
ondragover	onprogress
ondragstart	onratechange
ondrop	onreadystatechange
ondurationchange	onredo*

onemptied
onended
onerror
onfocus*
onformchange
onforminput
oninput
oninvalid
onkeydown
onkeypress
onkeyup
onload*
onloadeddata
onloadedmetadata
onloadstart

onresize*
onscroll
onseeked
onseeking
onselect
onshow
onstalled
onsubmit
onsuspend
ontimeupdate
onundo*
onunload*
onvolumechange
onwaiting

NOTE

onblur, onerror, onfocus, and onload behave slightly differently when applied to the body element because the body element shares these event handlers with its parent window.

---

*Event handler for Window object when used with the body element

Alphabetical List of Elements

This section contains a listing of all elements and attributes in HTML 4.01/XHTML 1.0 and HTML5, as well as a few non-standard elements.

Readers are advised to watch for these labels on elements and attributes:

Deprecated

Elements and attributes marked as ***Deprecated*** are being phased out of HTML—usually in favor of Cascading Style

Sheets—and are discouraged from use. All deprecated elements and attributes have been removed from the Strict versions of HTML 4.01 and XHTML 1.0.

HTML5 only
> Elements and attributes marked ***HTML5 only*** are new in HTML5 and may have limited or no browser support.

Not in HTML5
> Attributes marked ***Not in HTML5*** have been omitted from HTML5, usually because they are presentational or were never supported by popular browsers.

XHTML only
> Attributes marked ***XHTML only*** apply only to documents marked up in XHTML 1.0 or 1.1. Other minor differences between HTML and XHTML are noted similarly.

Nonstandard
> ***Nonstandard*** elements and attributes are not included in any version of the HTML or XHTML Recommendations but are well supported by browsers.

Required
> Attributes marked as ***Required*** must be included in the element for the markup to be valid.

---

a   **HTML 4.01 | HTML5**

`<a> . . . </a>`

Defines an *anchor* that can be used as a hypertext link or a named fragment within the document. When the `href` attribute is set to a valid URI, the anchor is a hypertext link to a web page, page fragment, or another resource. The `name` or `id` attributes are used to label an anchor and allow it to serve as the destination point of a link. An a element may have both `href` and `name`/`id` attributes.

Notes

In HTML5, the `href` attribute may be omitted to use an a element as a "placeholder link." HTML5 also permits flow content (block elements) within a elements.

Start/End Tags

Required/Required

Attributes

Core, Internationalization, Events, Focus, HTML5 Global Attributes

`charset="charset"`
> **Not in HTML5**. Specifies the character encoding of the target document.

`coords="x,y coordinates"`
> **Not in HTML5**. Specifies the x/y-coordinates for a clickable area in an image map. The HTML 4.01 Recommendation proposes that client-side image maps be replaced with an `object` element containing the image and a set of anchor elements defining the "hot" areas (with shapes and coordinate attributes). This system has not been implemented by browsers and has been dropped in HTML5.

`href="URI"`
> Specifies the location of the destination document or web resource (such as an image, audio, PDF, or other media file).

`hreflang="language code"`
> Specifies the base language of the target document.

`id="text"`
> Gives the link a unique name (similar to the `name` attribute) so that it can be referenced from a link, script, or style sheet. In XHTML, the `id` attribute is required for document fragments. For backward compatibility, authors use both `name` and `id` for fragments.

`media="all|aural|braille|handheld|print|projection|screen|tty|tv"`
> **HTML5 only**. Describes the media for which the target document was designed. The default is `all`.

`name="text"`
> **Not in HTML5**. *XHTML documents use* `id` *for document fragments*. Places a fragment identifier within an HTML document.

`ping="URLs"`

> **HTML5 only**. Specifies a list of URLs that must be contacted when the link is followed, useful for user tracking.

`rel="link type keyword"`

> Describes one or more relationships from the current source document to the linked document. The link types specified in both the HTML 4.01 and 5 specifications are `alternate`, `bookmark`, `help`, `index`, `next`, and `prev`. The HTML 4.01-only keywords include `appendix`, `chapter`, `contents`, `copyright`, `glossary`, `section`, `start`, and `subsection`. The following link types are specified in HTML5 only: `archives`, `author`, `external`, `first`, `last`, `license`, `nofollow`, `noreferrer`, `search`, `sidebar`, `tag`, and `up`.

`rev="link type keyword."`

> **Not in HTML5**. Specifies one or more relationships from the target back to the source (the opposite of the `rel` attribute).

`shape="rect|circle|poly|default"`

> **Not in HTML5**. Defines the shape of a clickable area in an image map. This part of HTML 4.01's proposal to replace client-side image maps with a combination of `object` and `a` elements. This system has not been implemented by browsers and was dropped in HTML5.

`target="text"`

> Specifies the name of the window or frame in which the target document should be displayed.

`type="MIME type"`

> Specifies the media or content type (MIME type) of the linked content—for example, `text/html`.

Examples

To a local file:

```
<a href="filename.html"> . . . </a>
```

To an external file:

```
<a href="http://server/path/file.html"> . . . </a>
```

To a named anchor:

```
<a href="http://server/path/file.html#fragment"> . . . </a>
```

To a named anchor in the current file:

```
<a href="#fragment"> . . . </a>
```

To send an email message:

```
<a href="mailto:username@domain"> . . . </a>
```

To a file on an FTP server:

```
<a href="ftp://server/path/filename"> . . . </a>
```

Creating a named anchor in HTML:

```
<a name="fragment"> . . . </a>
```

Creating a named anchor in XHTML (note that some authors also include a redundant name for backward compatibility with version 4 browsers):

```
<a id="fragment"> . . . </a>
```

---

abbr   HTML 4.01 | HTML5

```
<abbr> . . . </abbr>
```

Identifies the enclosed text as an abbreviation.

Start/End Tags

Required/Required

Attributes

Core, Internationalization, Events, HTML5 Global Attributes

title="*text*"
> Provides the full expression for the abbreviation. This may be useful for nonvisual browsers, speech synthesizers, translation systems, and search engines.

Example

```
<abbr title="Massachusetts">Mass.</abbr>
```

---

acronym

`<acronym>` . . . `</acronym>`

Indicates an acronym.

Notes

Not in HTML5. Authors are advised to use abbr instead.

Start/End Tags

Required/Required

Attributes

Core, Internationalization, Events

`title="text"`
> Provides the full expression for the acronym. This may be useful for nonvisual browsers, speech synthesizers, translation systems, and search engines.

Example

```
<acronym title="World Wide Web">WWW</acronym>
```

address   HTML 4.01 | HTML5

`<address>` . . . `</address>`

Supplies the author's contact information, typically at the beginning or end of a document. It is not to be used for all postal addresses, unless the address is provided as the contact information for the author of the document.

Notes

In HTML5, the address element may apply to a specific section or article within a document (as defined by the new section and article elements, respectively).

Start/End Tags

Required/Required

Attributes

Core, Internationalization, Events, HTML5 Global Attributes

Example

```
<address>
Contributed by <a href="http://example.com/authors
/robbins/"> Jennifer Robbins</a>, <a href="http://
www.oreilly.com/"> O'Reilly Media</a>
</address>
```

---

applet   HTML 4.01

`<applet> . . . </applet>`

Embeds a Java applet on the page. The `applet` element may contain a number of `param` elements that provide further instructions or parameters.

Notes

Deprecated (with all its attributes) in HTML 4.01 and XHTML 1.0.

Not in HTML5. In HTML5, this element and its attributes have been omitted entirely (in favor of `object`). The `applet` element is still supported by browsers and is expected to be for the foreseeable future. Some applets require the use of `applet`.

Start/End Tags

Required/Required

Attributes

Core

`align="left|right|top|middle|bottom"`
> Aligns the applet and allows text to wrap around it (same as image alignment).

`alt="text"`
> Provides alternate text if the applet cannot be displayed.

`archive="URLs"`
> Provides a space-separated list of URLs with classes to be preloaded.

code="*class*"
> ***Required***. Specifies the class name of the code to be executed.

codebase="*URL*"
> Specifies the URL from which the applet code is retrieved.

height="*number*"
> Specifies the height of the initial applet display area in pixels.

hspace="*number*"
> ***Deprecated***. Specifies the number of pixels of clear space to the left and right of the applet window.

name="*text*"
> ***Deprecated in XHTML 1.0***. Names the applet for reference from elsewhere on the page.

object="*text*"
> Names a resource containing a serialized representation of an applet's state. Use either code or object in an applet element, but not both.

vspace="*number*"
> ***Deprecated***. Specifies the number of pixels of clear space above and below the applet window.

width="*number*"
> ***Required***. Width of the initial applet display area in pixels.

Example

```
<applet code="Wacky.class" width="300" height="400">
  <param name="Delay" value="250">
  <param name="Time" value="120">
  <param name="PlaySounds" value="YES">
</applet>
```

---

area   **HTML 4.01 | HTML5**

HTML: <area>; *XHTML:* <area/> *or* <area />

The area element is used within the map element of a client-side image map to define a specific clickable ("hot") area.

Start/End Tags

This is an empty element. In HTML, the end tag is forbidden. In XHTML, the element must be closed with a trailing slash as just shown. Developers may include a space character before the slash for backward compatibility with older browsers.

Attributes

Core, Internationalization, Events, Focus, HTML5 Global Attributes

alt="*text*"

> **Required**. Specifies a short description of the image that is displayed when the image file is not available.

coords="*values*"

> Specifies a list of comma-separated pixel coordinates that define a "hot" area of an image map.

href="*URI*"

> Specifies the location of the document or resource that is accessed by clicking on the defined area.

hreflang="*language code*"

> **HTML5 only**. Specifies the language of the target document.

media="all|aural|braille|handheld|print|projection|screen|tty|tv"

> **HTML5 only**. Describes the media (e.g., screen, handheld, speech, print, etc.) for which the target document was designed. The default is all.

nohref="*nohref*"

> **Not in HTML5**. Defines a "mouse-sensitive" area in an image map for which there is no action when the user clicks in the area.

ping="*URLs*"

> **HTML5 only**. Specifies a list of URLs that have to be contacted when the link is followed, useful for user tracking.

rel="*relationships*"

> **HTML5 only**. Establishes one or more relationships between the current document and the target document in a space-separated list. Common relationships include stylesheet,

next, prev, copyright, index, and glossary (see a element listing for complete list of values.)

shape="rect|circle|poly|default"
: Defines the shape of the clickable area.

target="*text*"
: Specifies the name of the window or frame in which the target document should be displayed.

type="*MIME type*"
: Specifies the media or content type (MIME type) of the linked content—for example, text/html.

Example (HTML)

See also map.

```
<area shape="rect" coords="203,23,285,106" href=http://www.
nasa.gov alt="">
```

Example (XHTML)

```
<area shape="rect" coords="203,23,285,106" href=http://www.
nasa.gov alt="" />
```

---

article   HTML5

```
<article> . . . </article>
```

Represents a self-contained piece of content, such as a magazine article, blog post, reader comment, or other content that is intended to be independently distributable, reusable, or used in syndication. article elements may be nested, such as for comments associated with a blog post.

Notes

HTML5 only. The publication date or time of an article may be provided with the new time element with the pubdate attribute. See the time listing for more information.

Start/End Tags

Required/Required

Attributes

HTML5 Global Attributes

Example

```
<article>
  <header>
    <h1>Further Research</h1>
    <p><time pubdate datetime="2010-01-14T03:13"></time>
    </p>
    <p>An introduction to the topic. . .</p>
  </header>
  <p>Content of the article starts. . .</p>
  <p>And another paragraph in the article.</p>
  <footer>Copyright &#169; 2010 Jane Author</footer>
</article>
```

aside   HTML5

```
<aside> . . . </aside>
```

Represents content that is tangentially related to the surrounding content (a section, article, or other content flow), such as pull quotes, lists of links, advertising, and other content typically presented as a sidebar.

Notes

HTML5 only.

Start/End Tags

Required/Required

Attributes

HTML5 Global Attributes

Example

```
<article>
  <h1>Important Experiment Findings</h1>
  <p>First paragraph . . .</p>
  <p>Second paragraph . . .</p>
  <aside>
    <h1>For Further Reading</h1>
```

```
<ul>
  <li><a href="">Interesting Article</a></li>
  <li><a href="">Another Interesting Article</a></li>
</ul>
    </aside>
</article>
```

audio

`<audio> . . . </audio>`

Embeds a sound file media in the web page without requiring a plug-in. The content of the audio element can be used by agents that don't support the element.

Notes

HTML5 only. There is still debate regarding the supported audio format for the audio element (mainly open source Ogg Vorbis versus proprietary, yet more popular, formats such as .mp3). It is currently supported by Firefox 3.5+, Safari 3.2+, and Opera 10.0+. Chrome support is upcoming. Internet Explorer has not published plans to support audio.

Start/End Tags

Required/Required

Attributes

HTML5 Global Attributes

autobuffer *(or* autobuffer="autobuffer" *in XHTML5)*
> Tells the user agent (browser) that the media file is likely to be used and should be readily available

autoplay *(or* autoplay="autoplay" *in XHTML5)*
> Plays the media file automatically

controls *(or* controls="controls" *in XHTML5)*
> Indicates that the user agent (browser) should display a set of playback controls for the media file

loop *(or* loop="loop" *in XHTML5)*
> Indicates that the media file should start playing again automatically once it reaches the end

src="*URL*"
> Specifies the location of the media file

Examples

See also source.

```
<audio src="beachmusic.ogg" autoplay controls>
  This browser doesn't support <code>audio</code> elements.
</audio>
```

---

b

<b> . . . </b>

Renders the enclosed text in a bold font. Authors are advised to use the strong element when semantically correct.

Notes

In HTML5, the b element is slightly redefined as text that is emboldened without intending any extra importance, such as a keyword or a product name.

Start/End Tags

Required/Required

Attributes

Core, Internationalization, Events, HTML5 Global Attributes

Example

```
Turn left onto <b>Blackstone Blvd.</b>.
```

HTML: `<base>`; *XHTML:* `<base/>` *or* `<base />`

Specifies the base pathname for all relative URLs in the document. Place this element within the head of the document.

Start/End Tags

This is an empty element. In HTML, the end tag is forbidden. In XHTML, the element must be closed with a trailing slash as just shown. Developers may include a space character before the slash for backward compatibility with older browsers.

Attributes

`href ="URI"`

> ***Required in HTML 4.01.*** Specifies the absolute URI that acts as the base URI for resolving relative URIs.

`id="text"`

> ***XHTML and HTML5 only.*** Assigns a unique identifying name to the element.

`target ="name"`

> Defines the default target window for all links in the document.

Example (HTML)

```
<head>
    <title>Sample document</title>
    <base href="http://www.example.com/stories/">
</head>
```

Example (XHTML)

```
<head>
    <title>Sample document</title>
    <base href="http://www.example.com/stories/" />
</head>
```

basefont

HTML: `<basefont>`; *XHTML:* `<basefont/>` *or* `<basefont />`

Specifies certain font attributes for the content that follows it. It can be used within the head element to apply to the entire document or within the body of the document to apply to the subsequent text. This element is strongly discouraged from use in favor of style sheets for font control.

Notes

Deprecated in HTML 4.01 and XHTML 1.0. ***Not in HTML5***.

Start/End Tags

This is an empty element. In HTML, the end tag is forbidden. In XHTML, the element must be closed with a trailing slash as just shown.

Attributes

`id="text"`
> Assigns a name to an element. This name must be unique in a document.

`color="#rrggbb" or "color name"`
> ***Deprecated***. Sets the color of the following text.

`face="typeface" (or list of typefaces)`
> ***Deprecated***. Sets the font for the following text.

`size="number"`
> ***Deprecated***. Sets the base font size using size values from 1 to 7 (or relative values based on the default value of 3). Subsequent relative size settings are based on this value.

Example (HTML)

```
<head>
    <basefont face="Verdana, Helvetica, sans-serif">
</head>
```

Example (XHTML)

```
<head>
    <basefont face="Verdana, Helvetica, sans-serif" />
</head>
```

---

bdo

`<bdo>` . . . `</bdo>`

Stands for "bidirectional override" and is used to indicate a selection of text that reads in the opposite direction than the surrounding text. For instance, in a left-to-right reading document, the `bdo` element may be used to indicate a selection of Hebrew text that reads right to left (`rtl`).

Start/End Tags

Required/Required

Attributes

*Core, Events (**XHTML only**), HTML5 Global Attributes*

`dir="ltr|rtl"`
> ***Required***. Indicates whether the selection should read left to right (`ltr`) or right to left (`rtl`).

`lang="language code"`
> Specifies the language of the element using a language code abbreviation.

`xml:lang="text"`
> ***XHTML only***. Specifies languages in XML documents using a language code abbreviation.

Example

```
<bdo dir="ltr">English phrase in otherwise Arabic text.
</bdo>
```

big

`<big>` . . . `</big>`

By default, `big` sets the font size slightly larger than the surrounding text. This is an example of presentational HTML that should be avoided in favor of semantic markup and style sheets for presentation.

Notes

Not in HTML5.

Start/End Tags

Required/Required

Attributes

Core, Internationalization, Events

Example

```
Check out our <big>low prices</big>!
```

blockquote

`<blockquote>` . . . `</blockquote>`

Indicates a long quotation. Its content is some number of block-level elements, such as paragraphs.

Notes

In HTML5, the `blockquote` element is also a *sectioning root*, meaning it indicates a section that may have its own outline. That means that heading levels used within `blockquote` elements will not contribute to the overall outline of the page.

Start/End Tags

Required/Required

Attributes

Core, Internationalization, Events, HTML5 Global Attributes

```
cite="URI"
```
> Provides a link to information about the source from which
> the quotation was borrowed.

Example

```
<blockquote cite="http://www.example.com">
  <h1>Fascinating Evidence</h1>
  <p>This is the beginning of a lengthy quoted
      passage (text continues . . . ) </p>
  <p>And it is still going on and on
      (text continues . . . )</p>
</blockquote>
```

body   HTML 4.01 | HTML5

```
<body> . . . </body>
```

The body of a document contains the document's content. Content
may be presented visually (as in a graphical browser window) or
aurally (by a screen reader). There may only be one body element in
a document. In HTML documents, it is optional; in XHTML it is
required.

Notes

All of the presentational attributes for the body are deprecated in
(X)HTML and have been dropped from HTML5 in favor of style
sheet controls.

Start/End Tags

HTML 4.01 and 5: Optional/Optional; XHTML: Required/
Required

Attributes

Core, Internationalization, Events; plus onload and onunload

HTML5 Global Attributes; plus onafterprint, onbeforeprint,
onbeforeunload, onblur, onerror, onfocus, onhashchange, onload,
onmessage, onoffline, ononline, onpagehide, onpageshow,
onpopstate, onredo, onresize, onstorage, onundo, and onunload

```
alink="#rrggbb" or "color name"
```
> ***Deprecated. Not in HTML5***. Sets the color of active links (the
> color while the mouse button is held down during a click).

`background="`*`URL`*`"`

> ***Deprecated. Not in HTML5.*** Provides the location of a graphic file to be used as a tiling graphic in the background of the document.

`bgcolor="`*`#rrggbb`*`" or "`*`color name`*`"`

> ***Deprecated. Not in HTML5.*** Sets the color of the background for the document.

`link="`*`#rrggbb`*`" or "`*`color name`*`"`

> ***Deprecated. Not in HTML5.*** Sets the default color for all the links in the document.

`text="`*`#rrggbb`*`" or "`*`color name`*`"`

> ***Deprecated. Not in HTML5.*** Sets the default color for all the nonhyperlink and unstyled text in the document.

`vlink="`*`#rrggbb`*`" or "`*`color name`*`"`

> ***Deprecated. Not in HTML5.*** Sets the color of the visited links (links that have already been followed) for the document.

Example

```
<!DOCTYPE HTML PUBLIC "-//W3C//DTD HTML 4.01//EN"
 "http://www.w3.org/TR/HTML4.01/strict.dtd">
<html>
  <head>
    <title>Document Title</title>
  </head>
  <body>
    <p>Content of document . . . </p>
  </body>
</html>
```

---

br   HTML 4.01 | HTML5

HTML: `<br>`; *XHTML:* `<br/>` or `<br />`

Inserts a line break in the content, such as in a poem or postal address.

Start/End Tags

This is an empty element. In HTML, the end tag is forbidden. In XHTML, the element must be closed with a trailing slash as just shown. Developers may include a space character before the slash for backward compatibility with older browsers.

Attributes

Core, HTML5 Global Attributes

```
clear="none|left|right|all"
```
> ***Deprecated. Not in HTML5***. Specifies where the next line should appear after the line break in relation to floated elements (such as an image that has been floated to the left or right margin). The default, none, causes the next line to start where it would normally. The value left starts the next line below any floated objects on the left margin. Similarly, right starts the next line below floated objects on the right margin. The value all starts the next line below floats on both margins.

Example (HTML)

```
<p>O'Reilly Media<br>
1005 Gravenstein Highway North<br>
Sebastopol, CA 95472</p>
```

Example (XHTML)

```
<p>O'Reilly Media<br />
1005 Gravenstein Highway North<br />
Sebastopol, CA 95472</p>
```

---

button   HTML 4.01 | HTML5

```
<button> . . . </button>
```

Used as part of a form, defines a "button" that functions similarly to buttons created with the input element but allows for richer rendering possibilities. Buttons can contain content such as text and images (but not image maps).

Start/End Tags

Required/Required

Attributes

Core, Internationalization, Events, Focus, HTML5 Global Attributes

---

autofocus *(autofocus="autofocus" in XHTML)*

>   **HTML5 only**. Indicates the control should have focus (be highlighted and ready for user input) when the document loads.

disabled *(disabled="disabled" in XHTML)*

>   Disables the control for user input. It can be altered only via a script. Browsers may display disabled controls differently (grayed out, for example), which could be useful for dimming certain controls until required info is supplied.

form="*id of the form owner*"

>   **HTML5 only**. Explicitly associates the input control with its associated form (its *form owner*). With this method, the input control does not need to be a child of the form element that applies to it.

formaction="*URL*"

>   **HTML5 only**. Specifies the application that will process the form. It is used only with a submit button (input type="submit") and has the same function as the action attribute for the form element.

formenctype="*content type*"

>   **HTML5 only**. Specifies how the form values are encoded with the post method type. It is used only with a submit button (input type="submit") and has the same function as the enctype attribute for the form element. The default is Internet Media Type (application/x-www-form-urlencoded). The value multipart/form-data should be used in combination with the file input type.

formmethod="get|post|put|delete"

>   **HTML5 only**. Specifies which HTTP method will be used to submit the form data. It is used only with a submit button (input type="submit") and has the same function as the method attribute for the form element. The put and delete values are new in HTML5.

formnovalidate="*URL*"

>   **HTML5 only**. Indicates that the form is not to be validated during submission. It is used only with a submit button (input

type="submit") and has the same function as the novalidate attribute for the form element (new in HTML5).

formtarget="*name*"

HTML5 only. Specifies the target window for the form results. It is used only with a submit button (input type="submit") and has the same function as the target attribute for the form element.

name="*text*"

Required. Assigns the control name for the element.

type="submit|reset|button"

Identifies the type of button: submit button (the default type), reset button, or custom button (used with JavaScript), respectively.

value="*text*"

Assigns the value to the button control. The behavior of the button is determined by the type attribute.

Example

```
<button type="reset" name="reset"><img src="thumbs-down.
gif" alt="thumbs-down icon" /> Try again.</button>
```

---

canvas   HTML5

```
<canvas> . . . </canvas>
```

Represents a two-dimensional area that can be used for rendering dynamic bitmap graphics, such as graphs or games. The image on the canvas is generated with scripts.

Notes

HTML5 only.

The canvas element is one of the better supported HTML5 features, with basic support in Firefox 2.0+, Safari 3.1+, Chrome 1.0+, and Opera 9.0. Support is promised in Internet Explorer 9, but in the meantime, many developers use the ExplorerCanvas workaround (*excanvas.sourceforge.net*). A task force has been assembled to address the accessibility issues related to canvas to improve usability for the visually impaired.

Start/End Tags

Required/Required

Attributes

HTML5 Global Attributes

height="*number*"
> Specifies the height of the canvas area in CSS pixels.

width="*number*"
> Specifies the width of the canvas area in CSS pixels.

Example

```
<html>
<head>
   <script type="application/x-javascript">
function draw() {
  var canvas = document.getElementById("box");
  var ctx = canvas.getContext("2d");
  ctx.fillStyle = "rgb(163, 120, 240)";
  ctx.fillRect (55, 50, 75, 100);
}
   </script>
</head>
<body onload="draw()">
   <canvas id="box" width="250" height="250"></canvas>
</body>
</html>
```

---

caption   HTML 4.01 | HTML5

<caption> . . . </caption>

Provides a summary of a table's contents or purpose. The caption element must immediately follow the table start tag and precede all other table elements. The align attribute is deprecated in favor of the CSS caption-side property for caption positioning.

Note

In HTML5, if a table is in a dd element in a figure, use the dt element for the table caption instead.

Start/End Tags

Required/Required

Attributes

Core, Internationalization, Events, HTML5 Global Attributes

```
align="top|bottom|left|right"
```
Deprecated. *Not in HTML5*. Positions the caption relative to the table. The default position is top.

Example

See also table *listing.*

```
<table>
<caption>A brief description of the data in this
 table.</caption>
<tr>
    <td>data</td><td>data</td>
</tr>
</table>
```

---

center   HTML 4.01

```
<center> . . . </center>
```

Centers its contents horizontally in the available width of the page or the containing element. Use of this element is strongly discouraged in favor of style sheets for centering elements.

Notes

Deprecated in HTML 4.01/XHTML. ***Not in HTML5***.

Start/End Tags

Required/Required

Attributes

Core, Internationalization, Events

Example

```
<center>
    <h1>Introduction</h1>
    <p>Once upon a time . . . </p>
</center>
```

---

cite

`<cite> . . . </cite>`

Denotes the title of a work—a reference to another work, especially books, magazines, articles, and so on.

Start/End Tags

Required/Required

Attributes

Core, Internationalization, Events, HTML5 Global Attributes

Example

```
<p>Recipe from <cite>Food & Wine Magazine</cite>.</p>
```

---

code

`<code> . . . </code>`

Denotes a fragment of computer code that appears as an inline (phrasing) element.

Start/End Tags

Required/Required

Attributes

Core, Internationalization, Events, HTML5 Global Attributes

Example

```
<p>DOM reference: <code>document.getElementById</code></p>
```

HTML: `<col>`; *XHTML:* `<col/>` *or* `<col />`

Establishes a column (or columns via the `span` attribute) within a table so that attribute properties may be applied to all the cells in the column(s). The `col` element does not group columns structurally (that is handled by the `colgroup` element) but rather is an empty element that allows attributes to be shared. The `col` element must appear after the `caption` element and before any row (`tr`) or row group (`thead`, `tbody`, `tfoot`) elements with the `table` element.

Start/End Tags

This is an empty element. In HTML, the end tag is forbidden. In XHTML, the element must be closed with a trailing slash as just shown. Developers may include a space character before the slash for backward compatibility with older browsers.

Attributes

Core, Internationalization, Events, HTML5 Global Attributes

`align="left|right|center|justify|char"`
> **Not in HTML5**. Specifies the horizontal alignment of text in a cell or cells. The default value is `left`.

`char="character"`
> **Not in HTML5**. Specifies a character along which the cell contents will be aligned when `align` is set to `char`. The default character is a decimal point (language-appropriate). This attribute is generally not supported by current browsers.

`charoff="length"`
> **Not in HTML5**. Specifies the offset distance to the first alignment character on each line. If a line doesn't use an alignment character, it should be horizontally shifted to end at the alignment position. This attribute is generally not supported by current browsers.

`span="number"`
> Specifies the number of columns "spanned" by the `col` element. The default value is 1. All columns indicated in the span are formatted according to the attribute settings in `col`.

valign="top|middle|bottom|baseline"

> ***Not in HTML5***. Specifies the vertical alignment of text in the cells of a column.

width="*pixels, percentage, n**"

> ***Not in HTML5***. Specifies the width of each column spanned by the col element. Width can be measured in pixels or percentages, or defined as a relative size (*). For example, 2* sets the column two times wider than the other columns; 0* sets the column width at the minimum necessary to hold the column's contents. The width attribute in the col element overrides the width settings of the containing colgroup element.

Example (HTML):

See also colgroup *and* table.

```
<table>
<col span="2" width="100" class="name">
<col span="1" width="50" class="date">
<thead> . . . (markup continues)
```

Example (XHTML):

```
<table>
<col span="2" width="100" class="name" />
<col span="1" width="50" class="date" />
<thead> . . . (markup continues)
```

colgroup   HTML 4.01 | HTML5

```
<colgroup> . . . </colgroup>
```

Defines a conceptual group of columns that form a structural division within a table. The colgroup element must appear after the caption element and before any row (tr) or row group (thead, tbody, tfoot) elements with the table element.

A table may include more than one column group. The number of columns in a group is specified either by the value of the span attribute or by a tally of column (col) elements within the group. Column groups may be useful in speeding table display (for example, the columns can be displayed incrementally without waiting for the entire contents of the table) and provide a system for display on nonvisual display agents such as speech- and Braille-based browsers.

Start/End Tags

HTML 4.01: Required/Optional; HTML5: Optional/Optional; XHTML: Required/Required

Attributes

Same attributes as col element.

Example

See also table.

```
<table>
<colgroup id="employinfo">
   <col span="2" width="100" />
   <col span="1" width="50" class="date" />
</colgroup>
<thead> . . . (markup continues)
```

---

command   HTML5

HTML: <command>; *XHTML:* <command/> *or*

Used within a menu element, a command is an interactive element that represents an immediate action that can be triggered by the user (usually via onclick).

Notes

HTML5 only.

Start/End Tags

This is an empty element. It must be closed with a trailing slash in the XML serialization of HTML5.

Attributes

HTML5 Global Attributes

checked (checked="checked" *in XHTML5*)
    Indicates that a command is selected.

---

disabled *(disabled="disabled" in XHTML5)*
> Indicates that a command is not available in the current state.

icon="*URL*"
> Specifies the location of an image to be used as a button for the command.

label="*text*"
> Provides the name of the command, as displayed to the user.

radiogroup="*text*"
> Specifies the name of a group of commands when the command type is set to radio.

title="*text*"
> Provides a hint describing the command to aid the user.

type="command|checkbox|radio"
> Indicates the kind of command. The command keyword indicates a normal command with an associated action. checkbox indicates the command state can be toggled on or off. radio indicates the command represents the selection of one item from a list of items.

Example

```
<menu>
    <command onclick="cut()" label="Cut">
    <command onclick="copy()" label="Copy">
    <command onclick="paste()" label="Paste">
    <command onclick="delete()" label="Clear">
</menu>
```

(Comments)   HTML 4.01 | HTML5

```
<!-- ... -->
```

Inserts notes or scripts into the document that are not displayed by the browser. Comments can be any length and are not restricted to one line.

Start/End Tags

Required/Required

Attributes

Not applicable.

Example

```
<!-- start secondary navigation here -->
<ul> . . . (markup continues)
```

---

datalist

```
<datalist> . . . </datalist>
```

Used with an input control set to the new list type, the datalist element creates a drop-down menu of suggestions (via the option element), providing an "auto-complete" function as the user types in the field (also called a *combobox*). The difference between datalist and select is that the user does not need to select one of the suggestions and can write anything in the field.

Notes

HTML5 only.

Start/End Tags

Required/Required

Attributes

HTML5 Global Attributes

Example

```
<input type="text" list="flavors">
<datalist id="flavors">
  <option value="Vanilla">
  <option value="Chocolate">
  <option value="Mango">
</datalist>
```

`<dd> . . . </dd>`

Denotes the description portion of an item within a definition list (or *association list* as it is called in HTML5). The dd element must be used within the dl element and is preceded by either dt or dd. The dd element may contain other block-level elements.

Note

In HTML5, dd is also used to indicate the data within a figure element and the additional detailed information within a details element.

Start/End Tags

HTML: Required/Optional; XHTML: Required/Required

Attributes

Core, Internationalization, Events, HTML5 Global Attributes

Example

See dl, details, and figure.

---

del

HTML 4.01 | HTML5

`<del> . . . </del>`

Indicates deleted text. It may be useful for legal documents and any instance where edits need to be tracked. Its counterpart is the inserted text element (ins). The del element may be used to indicate either inline or block-level elements.

Start/End Tags

Required/Required

Attributes

Core, Internationalization, Events, HTML5 Global Attributes

`cite="`*`URL`*`"`

Can be set to point to a source document that explains why the document was changed.

`datetime="`*`YYYY-MM-DDThh:mm:ssTZD`*`"`

Specifies the date and time the change was made. Dates and times follow the format shown here where `YYYY` is the four-digit year, `MM` is the two-digit month, `DD` is the day, `hh` is the hour (00 through 23), `mm` is the minute (00 through 59), and `ss` is the second (00 through 59). TZD stands for Time Zone Designator, and its value can be `Z` (to indicate UTC, Coordinated Universal Time), an indication of the number of hours and minutes ahead of UTC (such as +03:00), or an indication of the number of hours and minutes behind UTC (such as –02:20).

This is the standard format for date and time values in HTML. For more information, see *www.w3.org/TR/1998/NOTE-date time-19980827*.

Example

```
Chief Executive Officer: <del title="retired" datetime=
"2010-08-01T14:09:00EDT">Peter Pan</del> <ins>Pippi
Longstocking</ins>
```

details   HTML5

`<details> . . . </details>`

Represents a disclosure widget (such as an area that can be toggled open and closed) that reveals additional information or controls. The `details` element may contain a `dt` element that provides a summary of the details and a `dd` element that provides the details themselves. The `details` element is not intended to be used for footnotes.

Notes

HTML5 only.

Start/End Tags

Required/Required

Attributes

HTML5 Global Attributes

open (open="open" *in XHTML5*)
> Specifies that the details should be in the open or revealed state when the document loads.

Example

```
<details>
  <dt>Bio information</dt>
  <dd>This is some information about the author the user
    might be interested in reading.</dd>
</details>
```

---

dfn   HTML 4.01 | HTML5

`<dfn> . . . </dfn>`

Indicates the defining instance of the enclosed term. It can be used to call attention to the introduction of special terms and phrases or to reference them later in the document.

Start/End Tags

Required/Required

Attributes

Core, Internationalization, Events, HTML5 Global Attributes

Example

```
<dfn>Truecolor</dfn> uses 24 bits per pixel.
```

---

dir   HTML 4.01

`<dir> . . . </dir>`

Creates a directory list consisting of list items (li). Directory lists were originally designed to display lists of files with short names, but they have been deprecated with the recommendation that unordered lists (ul) be used instead.

Notes

Deprecated in HTML 4.01/XHTML 1.0. ***Not in HTML5***.

Start/End Tags

Required/Required

Attributes

Core, Internationalization, Events, HTML5 Global Attributes

compact *(*compact="compact" *in XHTML)*
> ***Deprecated. Not in HTML5***. Makes the list as small as possible. Few browsers support the compact attribute.

Example

```
<dir>
  <li>index.html</li>
  <li>about.html</li>
  <li>news.html</li>
</dir>
```

---

div   HTML 4.01 | HTML5

`<div> . . . </div>`

Denotes a generic "division" within the flow of the document. Elements contained within a div are treated as a semantic group. The div element is typically given meaning with the class, id, title, or lang attributes, which also allow it to be accessible to scripts and selected in style sheets.

Start/End Tags

Required/Required

Attributes

Core, Internationalization, Events, HTML5 Global Attributes

align="center |left |right"
> ***Deprecated. Not in HTML5***. Aligns the text within the element to the left, right, or center of the page.

Example

```
<div id="summary">
  <h1>In Closing</h1>
  <p>We can summarize as follows...</p>
</div>
```

---

dl

```
<dl> . . . </dl>
```

Indicates a definition list. Each item in a definition list consists of two parts: a term (dt) and description (dd), which can represent terms and definitions or other name-value pairs. Within a dl, there should not be more than one dt element for each term, however, the dt may be followed by multiple dd elements.

Notes

In HTML5, the dl element has been slightly redefined as an "association list consisting of zero or more name-value groups (a description list)."

Start/End Tags

Required/Required

Attributes

Core, Internationalization, Events, HTML5 Global Attributes

```
compact="compact"
```
> **Deprecated. Not in HTML5.** Makes the list as small as possible. Few browsers support this attribute.

Example

```
<dl>
    <dt><code>em</code></dt>
    <dd>Indicates emphasized text.</dd>

    <dt><code>strong</code></dt>
    <dd>Denotes strongly emphasized text.</dd>
</dl>
```

```
<dt> . . . </dt>
```

Denotes the term portion of an item within a definition list. The
dt element may only include inline (phrasing) content.

Notes

In HTML5, the dt element is also used to provide a figure caption
within a `figure` element and the summary of details within a
`details` element.

Start/End Tags

HTML: Required/Optional; XHTML: Required/Required

Core, Internationalization, Events, HTML5 Global Attributes

Example

See dl, details, and figure.

```
<em> . . . </em>
```

Indicates emphasized text.

Start/End Tags

Required/Required

Attributes

Core, Internationalization, Events, HTML5 Global Attributes

Example

```
This is <em>exactly</em> what you've been looking for.
```

`<embed>` . . . `</embed>` *(or* `<embed />`*)*

Embeds an object into the web page. Embedded objects are most often multimedia files that use plug-in technology for playback (for example, Flash movies, QuickTime movies, and the like). In addition to the attributes listed below, certain media types and their respective plug-ins may have proprietary attributes for controlling the playback of the file.

Notes

Although commonly supported by browsers, the embed element was not part of the HTML 4.01 or earlier specifications (in favor of the object element for embedded media), however, it has been added to the HTML5 Working Draft. Because it was supported but not documented, it has many browser- and media-specific attributes and its syntax is not clear. Many developers use both object and embed for a single media object for backward compatibility, even though it does not conform to the HTML 4.01/XHTML standard.

Start/End Tags

There is conflicting documentation regarding whether embed is a container or an empty element. Modern browsers seem to support both methods, but including the closing tag is the safest bet. In HTML5, it is specified as an empty element.

HTML5 Attributes

HTML5 Global Attributes

height="*number*"

> Specifies the height of the object in number of pixels. Some media types require this attribute.

src="*URL*"

> Provides the location of the resource to be placed on the page.

width="*number*"

> Specifies the width of the object in number of pixels. Some media types require this attribute.

type="*media (MIME) type*"

> Specifies the MIME type of the media in order to load the appropriate plug-in. The suffix of the file name given as the source may also be used to determine which plug-in to use.

Nonstandard Attributes

These attributes are generally supported but were never included in an HTML specification:

align="left|right|top|bottom"

> Controls the alignment of the media object relative to the surrounding text. The default is bottom. While top and bottom are vertical alignments, left and right position the object on the left or right margin and allow text to wrap around it.

alt="*text*"

> Provides alternative text when the media object cannot be displayed (same as for the img element).

hidden="yes|no"

> Hides the media file or player from view when set to yes. The default is no.

hspace="*number*"

> Used in conjunction with the align attribute, the horizontal space attribute specifies (in pixels) the amount of space to leave clear to the left and right of the media object.

name="*text*"

> Specifies a name for the embedded object. This is particularly useful for referencing the object from a script.

palette="foreground|background"

> Applies to the Windows platform only. A value of foreground makes the plug-in's palette the foreground palette. Conversely, a value of background makes the plug-in use the background palette; this is the default.

pluginspage="*URL*"

> Specifies the URL for instructions for installing the appropriate plug-in.

`units="pixels|en"`

> Defines the measurement units used by `height` and `width`. The default is `pixels`. En units are half the point size of the body text.

`vspace="number"`

> Used in conjunction with the `align` attribute, the vertical space attribute specifies (in pixels) the amount of space to leave clear above and below the media object.

Internet Explorer only

`code="filename"`

> When the embedded object is a Java applet, specifies the class name of the Java code to be executed.

`codebase="URL"`

> Specifies the base URL for the application.

Netscape Navigator only

`pluginurl="URL"`

> According to Netscape, this "provides the URL of a Java Archive (JAR) file, which is a compressed collection of files that can be signed. The default plug-in invokes the JAR Installation Manager (JIM) with this JAR file URL, rather than loading the URL into a window. `pluginurl` takes precedence over `plugins` page. It is recommended that you use `pluginurl` rather than `pluginspage`."

Example with end tag

```
<embed src="movies/vacation.mov" width="240" height="196"
pluginspage="http://www.apple.com/quicktime/download/">
<noembed><img src="vacation.gif"> You do not seem to have
the plugin.</noembed>
</embed>
```

Example (HTML5)

```
<embed src="movies/vacation.mov" width="240" height="196"
type="video/quicktime">
```

```
<fieldset> . . . </fieldset>
```

Establishes a group of related form controls and labels. `fieldset` elements are placed within the `form` element. It is similar to `div` but is specifically for grouping form fields and inputs. It was introduced to improve form accessibility for users with alternative browsing devices.

Start/End Tags

Required/Required

Attributes

Core, Internationalization, Events, HTML5 Global Attributes

`disabled` *(disabled="disabled" in XHTML5)*
> **HTML5 only**. Disables the control for user input. It can be altered only via a script. Browsers may display disabled controls differently (grayed out, for example), which could be useful for dimming certain controls until required info is supplied.

`form="id of the form owner"`
> **HTML5 only**. Explicitly associates the input control with its associated form (its *form owner*). With this method, the input control does not need to be a child of the `form` element that applies to it.

`name="text"`
> **HTML5 only**. Assigns a name to the fieldset.

Example

```
<form>
<fieldset id="customer">
 <legend>Customer contact information</legend>
 <label>Full name <input type="text" name="name">
 </label>
  <label>Email Address <input type="text" name="email">
 </label>
  <label>State <input type="text" name="state"></label>
</fieldset>
</form>
```

figure

`<figure>` . . . `</figure>`

Indicates some set of self-contained content that is referred to from the main content, such as illustrations, code examples, diagrams, poems, and so on. The figure element may contain (in any order) one dd element that provides the figure content and, optionally, one dt element that provides the figure caption or title. If there is no dt element, the figure will have no caption.

Notes

HTML5 only.

Start/End Tags

Required/Required

Attributes

HTML5 Global Attributes

Examples

```
<figure>
   <dd><img src="tacocat.jpg" alt="a cat eating a taco">
   </dd>
</figure>

<figure>
<dt>Sample CSS rule</dt>
<dd>
   <pre>
body {
  background-color: #000;
  color: red;
}
   </pre>
</dd>
</figure>
```

figure | 57

font

`<font>` . . . `</font>`

An outdated method for affecting the style (color, typeface, and size) of the enclosed text. This element is no longer used in professional web design in favor of style sheets for changing text appearance.

Notes

Deprecated in HTML 4.01/XHTML 1.0; **Not in HTML5**.

Start/End Tags

Required/Required

Attributes

Core, Internationalization

`color="#RRGGBB"` or `"color name"`
> **Deprecated. Not in HTML5**. Specifies the color of the enclosed text.

`face="typeface"` *(or list of typefaces)*
> **Deprecated. Not in HTML5**. Specifies a typeface for the text. The specified typeface is used only if it is found on the user's machine. You may provide a list of fonts (separated by commas), and the browser will use the first available font in the string.

`size="value"`
> **Deprecated. Not in HTML5**. Sets the size of the type to an absolute value on a scale from 1 to 7 (3 is the default) or by using a relative value + *n* or - *n* (based on the default or basefont setting).

Example

```
<font face="serif" size="+1" color="red">Obsolete.</font>
```

footer

```
<footer> . . . </footer>
```

Represents information associated with a document, article, or section, such as copyright, publication date, author information, a list of related links, or other information typically found at the end of a document or section content.

Notes

HTML5 only.

Start/End Tags

Required/Required

Attributes

HTML5 Global Attributes

Examples

```
<article>
    <h1>How to Etch Glass</h1>
    <p>Start with clean glass...</p>
    ... markup continues...
    <footer>Copyright &copy; 2009 Jennifer Robbins</footer>
</article>
```

---

form

```
<form> . . . </form>
```

Indicates an interactive form that contains controls for collecting user input and other page content. There may be more than one form in a document, but forms may not be nested inside one another, and it is important that they do not overlap.

Start/End Tags

Required/Required

Attributes

Core, Internationalization, Events; plus onsubmit, onblur, onreset

---

`accept="`*`content-type-list`*`"`

> ***Not in HTML5***. Specifies a comma-separated list of file types (MIME types) that the server will accept and is able to process. One day browsers may be able to filter out unacceptable files when prompting a user to upload files to the server, but this attribute is not widely supported yet.

`accept-charset="`*`charset list`*`"`

> Specifies the list of character encodings for input data that must be accepted by the server to process the current form. The value is a space- and/or comma-delimited list of ISO character set names. The default value is `unknown`. This attribute is not widely supported.

`action="`*`URL`*`"`

> ***Required***. Specifies the URL of the application that will process the form. The default is the current URL.

`autocomplete="on|off"`

> ***HTML5 only***. Allows the user agent (browser) to fill in a field automatically (`on`) or requires the user to enter the information every time (`off`). Omitting this attribute causes the control to inherit the `autocomplete` setting for the associated `form` element.

`enctype="`*`content type`*`"`

> Specifies how the values for the form controls are encoded when they are submitted to the server when the method is post. The default is the Internet Media Type (`application/x-www-form-urlencoded`). The value `multipart/form-data` should be used in combination with the `file` input element.

`method="get|post"`

> Specifies which HTTP method will be used to submit the form data. With `get` (the default), the information is appended to and sent along with the URL itself.

`name="`*`text`*`"`

> ***Deprecated in XHTML 1.0***; *use* id *instead*. Assigns a name to the form.

---

novalidate (novalidate="novalidate" *in XHTML*)

> **HTML5 only**. Indicates that the form is not to be validated during submission.

target="*name*"

> Specifies a target for the results of the form submission to be loaded so that results of a form can be displayed in another window or frame. The special target values _bottom, _top, _parent, and _self may be used.

Example

```
<form action="/cgi-bin/guestbook.pl" method="get">
<p>First Name: <input type="text" name="first"></p>
<p>Nickname: <input type="text" name="nickname"></p>
<p><input type="submit" /> <input type="reset"></p>
</form>
```

---

frame   HTML 4.01

HTML: <frame>; *XHTML:* <frame/> *or* <frame />

Defines a single frame within a frameset.

Notes

Not in HTML5. The frameset, frame, and noframes elements are not included in HTML5.

Start/End Tags

This is an empty element. In HTML, the end tag is forbidden. In XHTML, the element must be closed with a trailing slash as just shown. Developers may include a space character before the slash for backward compatibility with older browsers.

Attributes

Core

frameborder="1|0"

> Determines whether there is a 3D separator drawn between the current frame and surrounding frames. A value of 1 turns the border on. A value of 0 turns the border off. The default value is 1 (border on).

`longdesc ="URL"`

>Specifies a link to a document containing a long description of the frame's contents. Although `longdesc` is included in the HTML 4.01 and XHTML 1.0 Recommendations, no browsers currently support it.

`marginheight="number"`

>Specifies the amount of space (in pixels) between the top and bottom edges of the frame and its contents. The minimum value according to the HTML 4.01 specification is 1 pixel. Setting the value to 0 to place objects flush against the edge of the frame works in some browsers but may yield inconsistent results.

`marginwidth="number"`

>Specifies the amount of space (in pixels) between the left and right edges of the frame and its contents. The minimum value according to the HTML specification is 1 pixel. Setting the value to 0 to place objects flush against the edge of the frame works in some browsers but may yield inconsistent results.

`name="text"`

>**Deprecated in XHTML 1.0**; *use* id *instead.* Assigns a name to the frame. This name may be referenced by targets within links to make the target document load within the named frame.

`noresize` (`noresize="noresize"` *in XHTML*)

>Prevents users from resizing the frame. By default, despite specific frame size settings, users can resize a frame by clicking and dragging its borders.

`scrolling="yes|no|auto"`

>Specifies whether scroll bars appear in the frame. A value of yes means scroll bars always appear, a value of no means scroll bars never appear, and a value of auto (the default) means scroll bars appear automatically when the contents do not fit within the frame.

`src="URL"`

>Specifies the location of the initial file or resource to be displayed by the frame.

Example

See `frameset`.

---

frameset HTML 4.01

`<frameset>` . . . `</frameset>`

Defines a collection of frames or other framesets. The `frameset` element is used in place of the `body` element for framed documents, and the document's DOCTYPE declaration should point to one of the Frameset DTDs as shown in the example below.

The `frameset` element may not contain any content but instead defines and names some number of frames (or other framesets) arranged in rows and/or columns. Each frame is indicated with a `frame` element within the `frameset`. A frameset document contains a regular header portion (as indicated with the `head` element).

Notes

Not in HTML5. `frameset`, `frame`, and `noframes` elements are not included in HTML5.

Start/End Tags

Required/Required

Attributes

Core, `onload`, `onunload`

`border="`*number*`"`
> ***Nonstandard***. Sets frame border thickness (in pixels) between all the frames in a frameset (when the frame border is turned on). Mozilla browsers do not support `border`.

`bordercolor="`*#rrggbb*`"` *or* `"`*color name*`"`
> ***Nonstandard***. Sets a border color for all the borders in a frameset. Mozilla and Opera browsers do not support `bordercolor`.

`cols="`*list of lengths*`"` *(number, percentage, or *)*
> Establishes the number and sizes of columns (vertical frames) in a frameset. The number of columns is determined by the

number of values in the list. Size specifications can be in absolute pixel values, percentage values, or relative values (*) based on available space.

frameborder="1|0"; "yes|no" *(Netscape)*

Nonstandard. Determines whether 3D separators are drawn between frames in the frameset. A value of 1 (or yes) turns the borders on; 0 (or no) turns the borders off. Netscape also supports values of 1 and 0. The Frameset DTD does not include the frameborder attribute for the frameset element.

rows="list of lengths" *(number, percentage, or *)*

Establishes the number and size of rows (horizontal frames) in the frameset. The number of rows is determined by the number of values in the list. Size specifications can be in absolute pixel values, percentage values, or relative values (*) based on available space.

Example

```
<!DOCTYPE HTML PUBLIC "-//W3C//DTD HTML 4.01 Frameset//EN"
 "http://www.w3.org/TR/HTML4.01/frameset.dtd">

<html>
<head>
<title>Simple Framed Document</title>
</head>


<frameset cols="200,*">
   <frame src="left.html">
   <frame src="right.html">
</frameset>

<noframes>
<body>
<p>Your browser does not support frames.</p>
</body>
</noframes>

</html>
```

`<hn > . . . </hn >`

Specifies a heading that briefly describes the section it introduces. There are six levels of headings, from h1 (most important) to h6 (least important). HTML syntax requires that headings appear in order (for example, an h2 should not precede an h1) for proper document structure. Doing so not only improves accessibility but aids in search engine optimization (information in higher heading levels is given more weight).

Note

In HTML5, heading order can be repeated within sections of the same document, allowing greater flexibility with heading levels. This is to aid the outlining of documents and allows sections of a document to fall into the outline correctly no matter which document the section appears in.

Start/End Tags

Required/Required

Attributes

Core, Internationalization, Events, HTML5 Global Attributes

`align="center|left|right"`
> ***Deprecated. Not in HTML5.*** Used to align the header left, right, or centered on the page.

Example

```
<h1>Story Title</h1>
<p>In the beginning . . .  </p>

<h2>Subsection Title</h2>
<p>And so on . . .  </p>
<p>And so on . . .  </p>
```

```
<head> . . . </head>
```

Defines the head portion of the document that contains information about the document. Every head element must include a `title` element that provides a description of the document. The head element may also include any of these elements in any order: base, link, meta, noscript, script, style, object (HTML 4.01 only), and command (HTML5 only). The head element merely acts as a container of these elements and does not have any content of its own.

Start/End Tags

HTML: Optional/Optional; XHTML: Required/Required

Attributes

Internationalization, HTML5 Global Attributes

```
id="text"
```
> ***XHTML and HTML5 only***. Assigns a unique identifying name to the element.

```
profile="URLs"
```
> ***Not in HTML5***. Provides the location of one or more predefined metadata profiles separated by whitespace that are used to define properties and values that can be referenced by meta elements in the head of the document, rel and rev attributes, and class names. This attribute is not well supported.

Example

```
<!DOCTYPE HTML PUBLIC "-//W3C//DTD HTML 4.01//EN"
  "http://www.w3.org/TR/HTML4.01/strict.dtd">
<html>
  <head>
    <title>Document Title</title>
    <style type="text/css">h1 {color: #333;}</style>
  </head>
  <body>
    <p>Content of document . . . </p>
  </body>
</html>
```

header HTML5

```
<header> . . . </header>
```

Represents information that goes at the beginning of a section, most often the headline, but the header may also include navigation links, advertising, introductions, etc. It may contain any flow content except header or footer elements.

Notes

HTML5 only.

Start/End Tags

Required/Required

Attributes

HTML5 Global Attributes

Examples

```
<body>
<header>
    <nav><ul><li>About</li><li>Home</li></nav>
    <h1>White Rabbits</h1>
    <p>Welcome to the White Rabbits fan site.</p>
</header>
<h2>Rabbit Sightings</h2>
... markup continues ...
</body>
```

hgroup HTML5

```
<hgroup> . . . </hgroup>
```

Used to group a stack of h1–h6 headings so that subsequent heading levels are treated as subheads or taglines and do not contribute to the outline structure of the page.

Notes

HTML5 only.

Start/End Tags

Required/Required

Attributes

HTML5 Global Attributes

Example

```
<hgroup>
  <h1>Web Design in a Nutshell</h1>
  <h2>A Desktop Quick Reference</h2>
</hgroup>
```

---

hr HTML 4.01 | HTML5

HTML: `<hr>`; *XHTML:* `<hr/>` *or* `<hr />`

Adds a horizontal rule to the page that can be used as a divider between sections of content. It is a block-level element.

Notes

This is an example of a presentational HTML element. In HTML5, this element is included but has been redefined as a "paragraph-level thematic break." Developers who want a purely decorative horizontal rule should opt for using style sheets to add a border on the top or bottom edge of a block element.

Start/End Tags

This is an empty element. In HTML, the end tag is forbidden. In XHTML, the element must be closed with a trailing slash as just shown. Developers may include a space character before the slash for backward compatibility with older browsers.

Attributes

Core, Internationalization, Events, HTML5 Global Attributes

`align="center|left|right"`
> ***Deprecated. Not in HTML5***. If the rule is shorter than the width of the window, this attribute controls horizontal alignment of the rule. The default is `center`.

---

noshade *(noshade="noshade" in XHTML)*
> ***Deprecated. Not in HTML5***. Displays the rule as a solid bar with no shading.

size="*number*"
> ***Deprecated. Not in HTML5***. Specifies the thickness of the rule in pixels.

width="*number*" *or* "*number%*"
> ***Deprecated. Not in HTML5***. Specifies the length of the rule in pixels or as a percentage of the page width. By default, rules are the full width of the browser window.

Example (HTML)

```
<p>These are notes from Thursday.</p>
<hr>
<p>These are notes from Friday.</p>
```

Example (XHTML)

```
<p>These are notes from Thursday.</p>
<hr />
<p>These are notes from Friday.</p>
```

html   HTML 4.01 | HTML5

```
<html> . . . </html>
```

This is the root element of HTML and XHTML documents, meaning all other elements are contained within it. The html element has no ancestors. The opening <html> tag is placed at beginning of the document, just after the document type declaration. The closing tag goes at the end of the document. In HTML, if the tags are omitted, html is still implied as the root element.

Start/End Tags

HTML: Optional/Optional; XHTML: Required/Required

Attributes

Internationalization, HTML5 Global Attributes

```
id="text"
```
> **XHTML and HTML5 only**. Assigns a unique identifying name to the element.

```
manifest="URL"
```
> **HTML5 only**. Points to a cache used with the offline web application API.

```
version="-//W3C//DTD HTML 4.01//EN"
```
> **Deprecated in HTML 4.01. Not in HTML5**. In HTML, the value of version is a Formal Public Identifier (FPI) that specifies the version of HTML the document uses (the value above specifies 4.01). In HTML 4.01, the version attribute is deprecated because it is redundant with information provided in the DOCTYPE declaration. In XHTML 1.0, the value of version has not been defined.

```
xmlns="http://www.w3.org/1999/xhtml"
```
> **Required for XHTML only**. In an XHTML document, this declares the XML namespace for the document.

Example (HTML)

```
<!DOCTYPE HTML PUBLIC "-//W3C//DTD HTML 4.01//EN"
 "http://www.w3.org/TR/HTML4.01/strict.dtd">
<html>
  <head>
    <title>Document Title</title>
  </head>
  <body>
    <p>Content of document . . . </p>
  </body>
</html>
```

Example (XHTML)

```
<!DOCTYPE html PUBLIC "-//W3C//DTD XHTML 1.0
Transitional//EN"
 "http://www.w3.org/TR/xhtml1/DTD/xhtml1-transitional
.dtd">
<html xmlns="http://www.w3.org/1999/xhtml" xml:lang="en"
lang="en">
  <head>
    <title>Document Title</title>
  </head>
  <body>
```

```
    <p>Content of document . . . </p>
  </body>
</html>
```

`<i> . . . </i>`

Enclosed text is displayed in italic. Authors are encouraged to use the more semantic em (emphasized) element when appropriate, or use style sheets to italicize semantically marked up text.

Notes

In HTML5, the i element is included and defined as a "span of text in an alternate voice or mood, or otherwise offset from normal prose...such as a technical term or idiomatic phrase from another language [or] some other prose whose typical typographic presentation is italicized."

Start/End Tags

Required/Required

Attributes

Core, Internationalization, Events, HTML5 Global Attributes

Example

```
The Western Black Widow Spider, <i>Latrodectus hesperus
</i>, is commonly found . . .
```

---

iframe   **HTML 4.01 | HTML5**

`<iframe> . . . </iframe>`

Defines an inline (floating) frame that is used for embedding an HTML document in a separate browsing context (window) within the parent document. An inline frame displays the content of an external document and may display scrolling devices if the content doesn't fit in the specified window area. Inline frames may be positioned similarly to images. The content of the iframe element

---

(between the start and end tags) displays in browsers that do not support inline frames.

Start/End Tags

Required/Required

Attributes

Core, HTML5 Global Attributes

align="top|middle|bottom|left|right"
> ***Deprecated. Not in HTML5***. Aligns the inline frame on the page within the flow of the text. Left and right alignment allows text to flow around the inline frame.

frameborder="1|0"
> ***Not in HTML5***. Turns on or off the display of a 3D border for the inline frame. The default is 1, which displays the border.

height="*number*"
> Specifies the height of the inline frame in pixels or as a percentage of the window size.

hspace="*number*"
> ***Nonstandard. Not in HTML5***. Used in conjunction with left and right alignment, this attribute specifies the amount of space (in pixels) to hold clear to the left and right of the inline frame.

longdesc="*URL*"
> ***Not in HTML5***. Specifies a link to a document containing a long description of the inline frame and its contents.

marginheight="*number*"
> ***Not in HTML5***. Specifies the amount of space (in pixels) between the top and bottom edges of the inline frame and its contents.

marginwidth="*number*"
> ***Not in HTML5***. Specifies the amount of space (in pixels) between the left and right edges of the inline frame and its contents.

name="*text*"

> **Deprecated in XHTML 1.0**. Assigns a name to the inline frame to be referenced by targeted links.

sandbox=" allow-same-origin|allow-forms|allow-scripts"

> **HTML5 only**. Used to disable or enable scripts, pop ups, plug-ins, and form submission in embedded documents.

scrolling="yes|no|auto"

> **Not in HTML5**. Specifies whether scroll bars appear in the frame. A value of **yes** means scroll bars always appear, a value of **no** means scroll bars never appear, and a value of **auto** (the default) means scroll bars appear automatically when the contents do not fit within the frame.

seamless *(seamless="seamless" in XHTML5)*

> **HTML5 only**. Makes the browser treat the embedded document as though it were part of the parent document for purposes of link targets, document structure, and CSS inheritance.

src="*URL*"

> Specifies the URL of the HTML document to display initially in the inline frame.

vspace="*number*"

> **Nonstandard. Not in HTML5**. Used in conjunction with left and right alignment, this attribute specifies the amount of space (in pixels) to hold clear above and below the inline frame.

width="*number*"

> Specifies the width of the inline frame in pixels or as a percentage of the window size. Internet Explorer and Navigator use a default width of 300 pixels.

Example

```
<h1>Inline (Floating) Frames</h1>
<iframe src="list.html" width="200" height="100"
scrolling="auto">
Your browser does not support inline frames. Read the list
  <a href="list.html">here</a>.
</iframe>
```

HTML: `<img>`; *XHTML:* `<img/>` *or* `<img />`

Places an image on the page. The `src` and `alt` attributes are required. Many attributes of the `img` element have been deprecated in favor of Cascading Style Sheets for presentation and positioning.

Start/End Tags

This is an empty element. In HTML, the end tag is forbidden. In XHTML, the element must be closed with a trailing slash as just shown. Developers may include a space character before the slash for backward compatibility with older browsers.

Attributes

Core, Internationalization, Events, HTML5 Global Attributes

`align="bottom|left|middle|right|top"`
> **Deprecated. *Not in HTML5***. Specifies the alignment of an image using one of the following values:

Value	Resulting alignment
bottom	Aligns the bottom of the image with the text baseline. This is the default vertical alignment.
left	Aligns the image on the left margin and allows subsequent text to wrap around it.
middle	Aligns the text baseline with the middle of the image.
right	Aligns the image on the right margin and allows subsequent text to wrap around it.
top	Aligns the top of the image with the top of the tallest object on that line.

`alt="text"`
> ***Required***. Provides a string of alternative text that appears when the image is not displayed. Browsers may display this text as a "tool tip" when the mouse rests on the image.

`border="number"`
> **Deprecated. *Not in HTML5***. Specifies the width (in pixels) of the border that surrounds a linked image.

`height="`*`number`*`"`

>   Specifies the height of the image in pixels. It is not required but is recommended to speed up the rendering of the web page.

`hspace="`*`number`*`"`

>   ***Deprecated. Not in HTML5***. Specifies (in number of pixels) the amount of space to leave clear to the left and right of the image.

`ismap` *(*`ismap="ismap"` *in XHTML)*

>   Indicates that the graphic is used as the basis for a server-side *image map* (an image containing multiple hypertext links).

`longdesc="`*`URL`*`"`

>   ***Not in HTML5***. Specifies a link to a long description of the image or an image map's contents. This may be used to make information about the image accessible to nonvisual browsers. It is not well supported.

`lowsrc="`*`URL`*`"`

>   ***Nonstandard***. Specifies an image (usually of a smaller file size) that will download first, followed by the final image specified by the `src` attribute. This was useful when dial-up Internet access was standard, but it is no longer commonly used.

`name="`*`text`*`"`

>   ***Deprecated in XHTML 1.0. Not in HTML5***. *Use id instead.* Assigns the image element a name so that it can be referred to by a script or style sheet.

`src="`*`URL`*`"`

>   ***Required***. Provides the location of the graphic file to be displayed.

`usemap="`*`URL`*`"`

>   Specifies the map containing coordinates and links for a *client-side image map* (an image containing multiple hypertext links).

`vspace="`*`number`*`"`

>   ***Deprecated. Not in HTML5***. Specifies (in number of pixels) the amount of space to leave clear above and below the image.

width="*number*"

 Specifies the width of the image in pixels. It is not required but is recommended to speed up the rendering of the web page.

Example (HTML)

```
<p>Your ideal pet: <img src="pig.gif" alt="A pig"></p>
```

Example (XHTML)

```
<p>Your ideal pet: <img src="pig.gif" alt="A pig" /></p>
```

---

input   HTML 4.01 | HTML5

HTML: `<input>`; *XHTML:* `<input/>` *or* `<input />`

The `input` element is used to create a variety of form input controls. The type of control is defined by the `type` attribute. Following is a complete list of attributes (with descriptions) that can be used with the `input` element. Not all attributes can be used with all control types. The attributes associated with each control type are listed below.

Notes

HTML5 adds a number of new values for the `type` attribute: `datetime`, `datetime-local`, `date`, `month`, `week`, `time`, `number`, `range`, `email`, `url`, `search`, and `color`. New HTML5 attributes for the `input` element are listed below.

Start/End Tags

This is an empty element. In HTML, the end tag is forbidden. In XHTML, the element must be closed with a trailing slash as just shown. Developers may include a space character before the slash for backward compatibility with older browsers.

Attributes

Core, Internationalization, Events, Focus; *plus* `onselect`, `onchange`, *HTML5 Global Attributes*

accept="*MIME type*"

 Specifies a comma-separated list of content types that a server processing the form will handle correctly. It can be used to

---

filter out nonconforming files when prompting a user to select
files to send to the server.

accesskey="*character*"

Assigns an *access key* (keyboard shortcut) to an element for
quicker access.

align="bottom|left|middle|right|top"

Deprecated. Not in HTML5. Specifies the alignment of an
image.

alt="*text*"

Specifies alternative text for an image used as a button.

autocomplete="on|off"

HTML5 only. Allows the user agent (browser) to fill in a field
automatically (on) or requires the user to enter the information
every time (off). Omitting this attribute causes the control to
inherit the autocomplete setting for the associated form
element.

autofocus *(autofocus="autofocus" in XHTML)*

HTML5 only. Indicates the control should have focus (be
highlighted and ready for user input) when the document
loads.

checked *(checked="checked" in XHTML)*

When this attribute is added to a radio button or checkbox
input, the input will be checked when the page loads.

disabled *(disabled="disabled" in XHTML)*

Disables the control for user input. It can be altered only via a
script. Browsers may display disabled controls differently
(grayed out, for example), which could be useful for dimming
certain controls until required info is supplied.

form="*id of the form owner*"

HTML5 only. Explicitly associates the input control with its
associated form (its *form owner*). With this method, the input
control does not need to be a child of the applicable form
element.

formaction="*URL*"

HTML5 only. Specifies the application that will process the
form. It is used only with a submit button (type="submit" or

"image") and has the same function as the `action` attribute for the `form` element.

`formenctype="content type"`

HTML5 only. Specifies how the form values are encoded with the `post` method type. It is used only with a submit button (`type="submit"` or `"image"`) and has the same function as the `enctype` attribute for the `form` element. The default is Internet Media Type (`application/x-www-form-urlencoded`). The value `multipart/form-data` should be used in combination with the `file` input type.

`formmethod="get|post|put|delete"`

HTML5 only. Specifies which HTTP method will be used to submit the form data. It is used only with a submit button (`type="submit"` or `"image"`) and has the same function as the `method` attribute for the `form` element. The `put` and `delete` values are new in HTML5.

`formnovalidate` (`formnovalidate="formnovalidate"` *in XHTML5*)

HTML5 only. Indicates that the form is not to be validated during submission. It is used only with a submit button (`type="submit"` or `"image"`) and has the same function as the `novalidate` attribute for the `form` element (new in HTML5).

`formtarget="name"`

HTML5 only. Specifies the target window for the form results. It is used only with a submit button (`type="submit"` or `"image"`) and has the same function as the `target` attribute for the `form` element.

`height="number of pixels"`

HTML5 only. Specifies the height of the button image when the input type is set to `image`.

`ismap` (`autofocus="autofocus"` *in XHTML*)

Not in HTML5. Indicates that the graphic is used as the basis for a server-side image map (an image containing multiple hypertext links). This attribute may be used with the "image" input type only.

`list="id of datalist"`

HTML5 only. Indicates that the control has a list of predefined suggestions for the user, which are provided by a `datalist` element. The value of the list attribute is the `id` of the associated `datalist`.

max="*number or string*"
> **HTML5 only**. Specifies the upper boundary of the accepted value range for the element. The `max` value must not be less than the `min` value.

maxlength="*number*"
> Specifies the maximum number of characters the user can enter for input elements set to `text`, `password`, `search`, `tel`, or `url`.

min="*number or string*"
> **HTML5 only**. Specifies the lower boundary of the accepted value range for the element. The `min` value defines the base for `step` operations.

multiple (multiple="multiple" *in XHTML*)
> **HTML5 only**. Indicates the user is allowed to specify more than one value.

name="*text*"
> **Required by all input types except `submit` and `reset`**. Assigns a name to the control; a script program uses this name to reference the control.

pattern="*JavaScript regular expression*"
> **HTML5 only**. Specifies a regular expression against which the control's value is to be checked. This is useful for making sure user input matches the format of the expected value, for example, a telephone number or an email address. The `title` attribute can be used with `pattern` to provide a description of the expected pattern/format of the input.

placeholder="*number*"
> **HTML5 only**. Provides a short (one word or short phrase) hint or example to help the user enter the correct data or format. If a longer description is necessary, use the `title` attribute.

readonly (readonly="readonly" *in XHTML*)
> Indicates that the form input may not be modified by the user.

required (required="required" *in XHTML*)
> **HTML5 only**. When present, indicates the input value is required.

size="*number*"

> Specifies the width of a text-entry control (when type is set to text, password, or search), measured in number of characters. Users may type entries that are longer than the space provided, causing the field to scroll to the right.

src="*URL*"

> When the input type is image, this attribute provides the location of the image to be used as a push button.

step="any/*number*"

> **HTML5 only**. Indicates the granularity that is expected and required of the value by limiting the allowed value to permitted units. The value of this attribute is dependent on the type of the input control. It may be a number, a text string (such as a date), or the keyword any, which allows any unit value.

tabindex="*number*"

> Specifies position in the tabbing order. Tabbing navigation allows the user to cycle through the active fields using the Tab key.

type="text|password|checkbox|radio|submit|reset|file|hidden| image|button" **New in HTML5:** "date|datetime|datetime-local| email|month|number|range|tel|time|url|week"

> Specifies the data type and associated form control. Descriptions of each input type and their associated attributes are listed below.

usemap="*URL*"

> **Not in HTML5**. Specifies the map containing coordinates and links for a client-side image map (an image containing multiple hypertext links). This attribute may be used with the "image" input type only.

value="*text*"

> Specifies the initial value for this control.

width="*number of pixels*"

> **HTML5 only**. Specifies the width of the bottom image when the input type is set to image.

---

input type="button"

Creates a customizable "push" button. Customizable buttons have no specific behavior but can be used to trigger functions created with JavaScript controls. Data from type="button" controls is never sent with a form when a form is submitted to the server; these button controls are for use only with script programs on the browser:

```
<input type="button" value="Push Me!">
```

Core, Internationalization, Events, Focus, HTML5 Global Attributes

align="left|middle|right|top|bottom" (***Deprecated. Not in HTML5.***)

autofocus (autofocus="autofocus" in XHTML) (***HTML5 only.***)

disabled (disabled="disabled" in XHTML)

form="*id of the form owner*" (***HTML5 only.***)

name="*text*" (***Required.***)

value="*text*"

input type="checkbox"

Creates a checkbox input element within a form. Checkboxes are like on/off switches that the user can toggle. Several checkboxes in a group may be selected at one time. When a form is submitted, only the "on" checkboxes submit values to the server:

```
<p>Which of the following operating systems have you
used?</p>
<ul>
<li><input type="checkbox" name="os" value="Win">Windows
</li>
<li><input type="checkbox" name="os" value="Linux"
    checked="checked">Linux</li>
<li><input type="checkbox" name="os" value="OSX"
    checked="checked">Macintosh OSX</li>
<li><input type="checkbox" name="os" value="DOS">DOS</li>
</ul>
```

Core, Internationalization, Events, Focus, HTML5 Global Attributes

align="left|middle|right|top|bottom" (***Deprecated. Not in HTML5.***)

autofocus (autofocus="autofocus" in XHTML) (***HTML5 only***) checked (checked="checked" in XHTML)

disabled (disabled="disabled" in XHTML)

form="*id of the form owner*" (**HTML5 only**)

name="*text*" (**Required**)

readonly (readonly="readonly" in XHTML)

required (required="required" in XHTML) (**HTML5 only**)

value="*text*" (**Required**)

input type="color"

This input type and its attributes are in HTML5 only.

Creates a color well control for selecting a color value:

```
<input type="color" value="3D458A">
```

HTML5 Global Attributes

autocomplete="on|off"

autofocus (autofocus="autofocus" in XHTML)

disabled (disabled="disabled" in XHTML)

form="*id of form owner*"

list="*id of datalist*"

name="*name*"

value="*text*"

input type="date"

This input type and its attributes are in HTML5 only.

Creates a date input control, such as a pop-up calendar, for specifying a date (year, month, day) with no time zone. The initial value must be provided in ISO date format:

```
<input type="date" name="birthday" value="2004-01-14">
```

HTML5 Global Attributes

autofocus (autofocus="autofocus" in XHTML)

autocomplete="on|off"

---

disabled (disabled="disabled" in XHTML)

form="*id of form owner*"

list="*id of datalist*"

max="*number or string*"

min="*number or string*"

name="*name*"

readonly (readonly="readonly" in XHTML)

required (required="required" in XHTML)

step="any|*number*"

value="*YYYY-MM-DD*"

input type="datetime"

This input type and its attributes are in HTML5 only.

Creates a combined date/time input control. The value is an ISO formatted date and time that is defined and submitted as UTC time (equivalent to GMT):

```
<input type="datetime" name="post" value=
"2004-01-14T18:05:32:00Z">
```

HTML5 Global Attributes

autocomplete="on|off"

autofocus (autofocus="autofocus" in XHTML)

disabled (disabled="disabled" in XHTML)

form="*id of form owner*"

list="*id of datalist*"

max="*number or string*"

min="*number or string*"

name="*name*"

readonly (readonly="readonly" in XHTML)

required (required="required" in XHTML)

step="any|*number*"

```
value="YYYY-MM-DDThh:mm:ssTZD"
```

input type="datetime-local"
*This input type and its attributes are in **HTML5** only.*

Creates a combination date/time input control, assuming the time
is in the local time zone. Initial values must be provided in ISO date/
time format:

```
<input type="datetime-local" name="post" value=
"2009-06-23T13:44:16:00">
```

HTML5 Global Attributes

```
autocomplete="on|off"
```

```
autofocus (autofocus="autofocus" in XHTML)
```

```
disabled (disabled="disabled" in XHTML)
```

```
form="id of form owner"
```

```
list="id of datalist"
```

```
max="number or string"
```

```
min="number or string"
```

```
name="name"
```

```
readonly (readonly="readonly" in XHTML)
```

```
required (required="required" in XHTML)
```

```
step="any|number"
```

```
value="YYYY-MM-DDThh:mm:ss"
```

input type="email"
*This input type and its attributes are in **HTML5** only.*

Creates a text input for entering one or more email addresses. The
user agent may look for patterns to confirm the entry is in email
address format:

```
<input type="email" name="post" value="jan@example.com">
```

HTML5 Global Attributes

```
autocomplete="on|off"
```

autofocus (autofocus="autofocus" in XHTML)

disabled (disabled="disabled" in XHTML)

form="*id of form owner*"

list="*id of datalist*"

maxlength="*number*"

multiple (multiple="multiple" in XHTML)

pattern="*JavaScript regular expression*"

placeholder="*text*"

name="*name*"

readonly (readonly="readonly" in XHTML)

required (required="required" in XHTML)

size="*number*"

value="*text*"

input type="file"

Allows users to submit external files with their form submissions
by providing a browsing mechanism in the form:

```
<form enctype="multipart/form-data">
<p>Send this file with my form information:<br>
<input type="file" name="attachment" size="28">
</p>
</form>
```

Core, Internationalization, Events, Focus, HTML5 Global Attributes

accept="*MIME type*"

autofocus (autofocus="autofocus" in XHTML) (**HTML 5 only**)

disabled (disabled="disabled" in XHTML)

form="*id of form owner*" (**HTML 5 only**)

maxlength="*number*"

multiple (multiple="multiple" in XHTML) (**HTML 5 only**)

name="*text*" (**Required**)

readonly (readonly="readonly" in XHTML)

required (required="required" in XHTML) (**HTML 5 only**)

size="*number*"

value="*text*"

input type="hidden"

Creates a control that does not display in the browser. Hidden controls can be used to pass special form-processing information to the server that the user cannot see or alter:

```
<input type="hidden" name="productID" value="12-XL">
```

HTML5 Global Attributes

accesskey="*character*"

disabled (disabled="disabled" in XHTML) (**HTML 5 only**)

form="*id of form owner*" (**HTML 5 only**)

name="*text*" (**Required**)

tabindex="*number*" (**Not in HTML5**)

value="*text*" (**Required**)

input type="image"

Allows an image to be used as a substitute for a submit button. If a type="image" button is pressed, the form is submitted:

```
<input type="image" src="graphics/sendme.gif" alt="Send me">
```

Core, Internationalization, Events, Focus, HTML5 Global Attributes

align="top|middle|bottom" (**Not in HTML5**)

alt="*text*" (**Not in HTML5**)

autofocus (autofocus="autofocus" in XHTML) (**HTML 5 only**)

disabled (disabled="disabled" in XHTML)

form="*id of form owner*" (**HTML 5 only**)

formaction="*URL*" (**HTML 5 only**)

formenctype="*content type*" (**HTML 5 only**)

formmethod="get|post|put|delete" (**HTML 5 only**)

---

formnovalidate (formnovalidate="formnovalidate" in XHTML) (**HTML 5 only**)

formtarget="*name*" (**HTML 5 only**)

height="*number of pixels*" (**HTML5 only**)

ismap (ismap="ismap" in XHTML)

name="*text*"

src="*URL*"

usemap="*URL*"

width="*number of pixels*" (**HTML5 only**)

input type="month"

This input type and its attributes are in HTML5 only.

Creates a date input control, such as a pop-up calendar, for specifying a particular month in a year:

```
<input type="month" value="2009-09" name="expires">
```

HTML5 Global Attributes

autocomplete="on|off"

autofocus (autofocus="autofocus" in XHTML)

disabled (disabled="disabled" in XHTML)

form="*id of form owner*"

list="*id of datalist*"

max="*number or string*"

min="*number or string*"

name="*name*"

readonly (readonly="readonly" in XHTML)

required (required="required" in XHTML)

step="any|*number*"

value="*YYYY-MM*"

input type="number"

This input type and its attributes are in HTML5 only.

Creates a control (a text field or spinner) for specifying a numerical value:

```
<input type="number" name="price" minimum="100000"
max="1000000" step="10000">
```

HTML5 Global Attributes

autocomplete="on|off"

autofocus (autofocus="autofocus" in XHTML)

disabled (disabled="disabled" in XHTML)

form="*id of form owner*"

list="*id of datalist*"

max="*number*"

min="*number*"

name="*name*"

readonly (readonly="readonly" in XHTML)

required (required="required" in XHTML)

step="any|*number*"

value="*text or number string*"

input type="password"

Creates a text input element (like <input type="text">), but the input text is rendered in a way that hides the characters, such as by displaying a string of asterisks or bullets. Note that this does *not* encrypt the information entered and should not be considered to be a real security measure:

```
<input type="password" name="password" size="8"
maxlength="8" value="abcdefg">
```

Core, Internationalization, Events, Focus, HTML5 Global Attributes

autocomplete="on|off" (***HTML5 only***)

autofocus (autofocus="autofocus" in XHTML) (***HTML5 only***)

---

disabled (disabled="disabled" in XHTML)

form="*id of form owner*" (**HTML5 only**)

maxlength="*number*"

name="*text*" (**Required**)

pattern="*JavaScript regular expression*" (**HTML5 only**)

placeholder="*text*" (**HTML5 only**)

readonly (readonly="readonly" in XHTML)

required (required="required" in XHTML) (**HTML5 only**)

size="*number*"

value="*text*"

input type="radio"

Creates a radio button that can be turned on and off. When a number of radio buttons share the same control name, only one button within the group can be "on" at one time, and all the others are "off." This makes them different from checkboxes, which allow multiple choices to be selected within a group. Only data from the "on" radio button is sent when the form is submitted:

```
<p>Which of the following operating systems do you like
best?</p>
<ul>
<li><input type="radio" name="os" value="Win">Windows</li>
<li><input type="radio" name="os" value="Linux">Linux</li>
<li><input type="radio" name="os" value="OSX" checked>
Macintosh OSX</li>
<li><input type="radio" name="os" value="DOS">DOS</li>
</ul>
```

Core, Internationalization, Events, Focus, HTML5 Global Attributes

checked (checked="checked" in XHTML)

autofocus (autofocus="autofocus" in XHTML) (**HTML5 only**)

disabled (disabled="disabled" in XHTML)

form="*id of form owner*" (**HTML5 only**)

name="*text*" (**Required**)

readonly (readonly="readonly" in XHTML)

required (required="required" in XHTML) (**HTML5 only**)

value="*text*" (***Required***)

input type="range"

This input type and its attributes are in HTML5 only.

Creates a slider control that a user can employ to enter a value that does not need to be precise. The range starts at the value provided by the min attribute (0 by default) and ends at the value provided by the max attribute (100 by default):

```
<input type="range" name="satisfaction" min="0" max="10">
```

HTML5 Global Attributes

autocomplete="on|off"

autofocus (autofocus="autofocus" in XHTML)

disabled (disabled="disabled" in XHTML)

form="*id of form owner*"

list="*id of datalist*"

max="*number*"

min="*number*"

name="*name*"

step="any|*number*"

value="*text*"

input type="reset"

Creates a reset button that clears the contents of the elements in a form (or sets them to their default values):

```
<input type="reset" value="Start Over">
```

Core, Internationalization, Events, Focus, HTML5 Global Attributes

autofocus (autofocus="autofocus" in XHTML) (**HTML5 only**)

disabled (disabled="disabled" in XHTML)

form="*id of form owner*" (**HTML5 only**)

name="*text*"

---

value="*text*"

input type="search"

This input type and its attributes are in HTML5 only.

Creates a one-line text input control for entering a search query:

```
<input type="search" name="srch" size="25"
value="Search term">
```

HTML5 Global Attributes

autocomplete="on|off"

autofocus (autofocus="autofocus" in XHTML)

disabled (disabled="disabled" in XHTML)

form="*id of form owner*"

list="*id of datalist*"

maxlength="*number*"

pattern="*JavaScript regular expression*"

placeholder="*text*"

name="*name*"

readonly (readonly="readonly" in XHTML)

required (required="required" in XHTML)

size="*number*"

value="*text*"

input type="submit"

Creates a submit button control. Pressing the button immediately sends the information in the form to the server for processing:

```
<p>You have completed the form.</p>
<p><input type="submit"></p>
```

Core, Internationalization, Events, Focus, HTML5 Global Attributes

autofocus (autofocus="autofocus" in XHTML) (***HTML 5 only***)

disabled (disabled="disabled" in XHTML)

form="*id of form owner*" (***HTML 5 only***)

formaction="*URL*" (**HTML 5 only**)

formenctype="*content type*" (**HTML 5 only**)

formmethod="get|post|put|delete" (**HTML 5 only**)

formnovalidate (formnovalidate="formnovalidate" in XHTML) (**HTML 5 only**)

formtarget="*name*" (**HTML 5 only**)

name="*text*"

value="*text*"

input type="tel"

This input type and its attributes are in HTML5 only.

Creates an input control for entering and editing a telephone number:

```
<input type="tel" name="homeno" value="123-555-2000">
```

HTML5 Global Attributes

autocomplete="on|off"

autofocus (autofocus="autofocus" in XHTML)

disabled (disabled="disabled" in XHTML)

form="*id of form owner*"

list="*id of datalist*"

maxlength="*number*"

pattern="*JavaScript regular expression*"

placeholder="*text*"

name="*name*"

readonly (readonly="readonly" in XHTML)

required (required="required" in XHTML)

size="*number*"

value="*text*"

input type="text"

Creates a text input element. This is the default input type, as well as one of the most useful and common. Text provided for the value attribute will appear in the text control when the form loads:

```
<input type="text" name="name" size="15" maxlength="50"
value="enter your name">
```

Core, Internationalization, Events, Focus, HTML5 Global Attributes

autocomplete="on|off" (***HTML5 only***)

autofocus (autofocus="autofocus" in XHTML) (***HTML 5 only***)

disabled (disabled="disabled" in XHTML)

form="*id of form owner*" (***HTML 5 only***)

list="*id of datalist*" (***HTML5 only***)

maxlength="*number*"

name="*text*" (***Required***)

pattern="*JavaScript regular expression*" (***HTML5 only***)

placeholder="*text*" (***HTML5 only***)

readonly (readonly="readonly" in XHTML)

required (required="required" in XHTML) (***HTML5 only***)

size="*number*"

value="*text*"

input type="time"
This input type and its attributes are in HTML5 only.

Creates a date input control for specifying a time (hour, minute, seconds, fractional seconds) with no time zone indicated:

```
<input type="time" name="currenttime" value="23:15:00">
```

HTML5 Global Attributes

autocomplete="on|off"

autofocus (autofocus="autofocus" in XHTML)

disabled (disabled="disabled" in XHTML)

```
form="id of form owner"

list="id of datalist"

max="number or string"

min="number or string"

name="name"

readonly (readonly="readonly" in XHTML)

required (required="required" in XHTML)

step="any|number"

value="hh:mm:ss"
```

input type="url"

This input type and its attributes are in HTML5 only.

Creates a text entry control for entering a single absolute URL. The user agent may validate the data entered to ensure it is in proper URL format and return an error message if it doesn't match:

```
<input type="url" name="blog" size="25"
value="http://www.example.com">
```

HTML5 Global Attributes

```
autocomplete="on|off"
```

autofocus (autofocus="autofocus" in XHTML)

disabled (disabled="disabled" in XHTML)

```
form="id of form owner"

list="id of datalist"

maxlength="number"

pattern="JavaScript regular expression"

placeholder="text"

name="name"
```

readonly (readonly="readonly" in XHTML)

required (required="required" in XHTML)

```
size="number"
```

value="*text*"

input type="week"

This input type and its attributes are in HTML5 only.

Creates a date input control, such as a pop-up calendar, for specifying a particular week in a year. Values are provided in ISO week numbering format:

```
<input type="week" name="thisweek" value="2009-W34">
```

HTML5 Global Attributes

autocomplete="on|off"

autofocus (autofocus="autofocus" in XHTML)

disabled (disabled="disabled" in XHTML)

form="*id of form owner*"

list="*id of datalist*"

max="*number or string*"

min="*number or string*"

name="*name*"

readonly (readonly="readonly" in XHTML)

required (required="required" in XHTML)

step="any|*number*"

value="*YYYY-W#*"

---

ins

```
<ins> . . . </ins>
```

Indicates text that has been inserted into the document. It may be useful for legal documents and any instance in which edits need to be tracked. Its counterpart is deleted text (del). The ins element may indicate either inline or block-level elements; however, when used as an inline element (as within a p), it may not insert block-level elements because that would violate nesting rules.

Start/End Tags

Required/Required

Attributes

Core, Internationalization, Events, HTML5 Global Attributes

`cite="URL"`

Can be set to point to a source document that explains why the document was changed.

`datetime="YYYY-MM-DDThh:mm:ssTZD"`

Specifies the date and time the change was made. See `del` for an explanation of the date/time format.

Example

```
<li>Chief Executive Officer: <del title="retired">Peter Pan
</del> <ins>Pippi Longstocking</ins></li>
```

---

isindex

HTML: `<isindex>`; *XHTML:* `<isindex/>` *or* `<isindex />`

Marks the document as searchable. The server on which the document is located must have a search engine that supports this searching. The browser displays a text entry field and a generic line that says, "This is a searchable index. Enter search keywords." The `isindex` element is not part of the form system and does not need to be contained within a `form` element.

Notes

Deprecated in HTML 4.01/XHTML 1.0. **Not in HTML5**. This method is outdated; more sophisticated searches can be handled with form elements.

Start/End Tags

This is an empty element. In HTML, the end tag is forbidden. In XHTML, the element must be closed with a trailing slash as just shown. Developers may include a space character before the slash for backward compatibility with older browsers.

Attributes

Core, Internationalization

prompt="*text*"
> Provides alternate text (not the default) to be used as a query by the user.

Example

    <isindex prompt="Enter your search term">

---

kbd

<kbd> . . . </kbd>

Stands for "keyboard" and indicates text (or voice input) entered by the user.

Start/End Tags

Required/Required

Attributes

Core, Internationalization, Events, HTML5 Global Attributes

Example

    <p>Enter your coupon code. Example: <kbd>AX4003</kbd></p>

---

keygen

HTML: <keygen>; *XHMTL:* <keygen/> *or*

Used as part of a form to generate key pairs that are used in web-based certificate management systems (for secure transactions).

Notes

HTML5 only.

Start/End Tags

This is an empty element. It must be closed with a trailing slash in XHTML5 documents. Developers may include a space character before the slash for backward compatibility with older browsers.

Attributes

HTML5 Global Attributes

autofocus (autofocus="autofocus" *in XHTML5*)
Indicates the control should be active and ready for user input when the document loads.

challenge="*challenge-string*"
Provides a challenge string to be submitted with the key.

disabled (disabled="disabled" *in XHTML5*)
Prevents the control from being interactive and prevents its value from being submitted.

form="*id of form owner*"
Associates the element with a named form on the page.

keytype="*keyword*"
Identifies the type of key to be generated, for example, rsa or ec.

name="*text*"
Gives the control an identifying name for the form submission process.

Example

The following is based on an example from *developer.mozilla.org*, used with permission via a Creative Commons "Attribution-Share Alike" License:

```
<form method="post" action="http://www.example.com/cgi-bin/
decode.cgi">
    <keygen name="RSA public key" challenge="123456789"
        keytype="RSA">
    <input type="submit" name="createcertificate"
        value="Make Key">
</form>
```

```
<label> . . . </label>
```

Used to attach information to controls. Each label element is associated with exactly one form control. The label element may contain the form control, or it may use the for attribute to identify the control by its id value.

Notes

In HTML5, a label may contain the input and use the for/id method.

Start/End Tags

Required/Required

Attributes

Core, Internationalization, Events, Focus, HTML5 Global Attributes

for="*text*"
:   Explicitly associates the label with the control by matching the value of the for attribute with the value of the id attribute within the control element.

form="*id of the form owner*"
:   Explicitly associates the label element with its associated form (its *form owner*). With this method, the label does not need to be the child of the applicable form element.

Examples

Form control and its labeling text contained within the label element:

```
<label>Last Name: <input type="text" size="32"></label>
```

Using the for/id method to associate the form control with its labeling text:

```
<label for="lastname">Last Name:</label>
<input type="text" id="lastname" size="32">
```

legend HTML 4.01 | HTML5

```
<legend> . . . </legend>
```

Assigns a caption to a fieldset (it must be the first child of a field set element). This improves accessibility when the fieldset is rendered nonvisually.

Start/End Tags

Required/Required

Attributes

Core, Internationalization, Events, HTML5 Global Attributes

```
accesskey="character"
```
> Assigns an access key (keyboard shortcut) to an element for quicker access.

```
align="top|bottom|left|right"
```
> **Deprecated. Not in HTML5.** Aligns the text relative to the fieldset.

Example

```
<fieldset>
  <legend>Mailing List Sign-up</legend>
  <ul>
  <li><label>Add me to your mailing list
        <input type="radio" name"list"></label></li>
  <li><label>No thanks <input name"list" value="no">
        </label></li>
    </ul>
</fieldset>
```

li HTML 4.01 | HTML5

```
<li> . . . </li>
```

Defines an item in a list. It is used within the ol, ul, menu, and dir list elements. (Note that menu and dir are deprecated in HTML 4.01. In HTML5, menu has been redefined and dir has been removed.)

Start/End Tags

HTML: Required/Optional; XHTML: Required/Required

Attributes

Core, Internationalization, Events, HTML5 Global Attributes

type="*format*"
> **Deprecated. Not in HTML5**. Changes the format of the au-
> tomatically generated numbers or bullets for list items.
>
> Within unordered lists (ul), the type attribute can be used to
> specify the bullet style (disc, circle, or square) for a particular
> list item.
>
> Within ordered lists (ol), the type attribute specifies the num-
> bering style for a particular list item (see options under the
> ol listing).

start="*number*"
> **Nonstandard**. Within ordered lists, you can specify the first
> number in the number sequence. In the (X)HTML Recom-
> mendations, the start attribute applies to the ol element, not
> li.

value="*number*"
> **Deprecated in HTML 4.01. Included in HTML5**. Within
> ordered lists, specifies an item's number. Following list items
> increase from the specified number.

Example

```
<ol>
  <li>Preheat oven to 300.</li>
  <li>Wrap garlic in foil.</li>
  <li>Bake for 2 hours.</li>
</ol>
```

link   HTML 4.01 | HTML5

HTML: <link>; *XHTML:* <link/> *or* <link />

Defines the relationship between the current document and another
document. Although it can signify such relationships as index, next,

and previous, it is most often used to link a document to an external style sheet.

Start/End Tags

This is an empty element. In HTML, the end tag is forbidden. In XHTML, the element must be closed with a trailing slash as just shown. Developers may include a space character before the slash for backward compatibility with older browsers.

Attributes

Core, Internationalization, Events, HTML5 Global Attributes

charset="*charset*"
> **Not in HTML5**. Specifies the character encoding of the linked document.

href="*URL*"
> Identifies the linked document.

hreflang="*language code*"
> Specifies the base language of the linked document.

media="all|screen|print|handheld|projection|tty|tv|projec
tion|braille|aural"
> Identifies the media to which the linked resource applies. Most often, it is used to assign style sheets to their appropriate media.

rel="*link type keyword*"
> Describes one or more relationships from the current source document to the linked document. The link types specified in both the HTML 4.01 and 5 specifications are alternate, help, index, next, prev, and stylesheet. The HTML 4.01-only keywords include appendix, chapter, contents, copyright, glossary, section, start, and subsection. The following link types are specified in HTML5 only: archives, author, first, icon, last, license, pingback, prefetch, search, sidebar, tag, and up.

rev="*relationships*"
> **Not in HTML5**. Specifies one or more relationship of the linked document back to the source (the opposite of the rel attribute).

---

sizes="any|*two pixel measurements*"

> **HTML5 only**. Specifies a size when the rel of the link is set to icon.

target ="*name*"

> **Not in HTML5**. Defines the default target window for all links in the document. Often used to target frames.

title ="*name*"

> **HTML5 only**. Provides the title of the linked resource.

type="*resource*"

> Shows the media or content type of a linked resource. The value text/css indicates that the linked document is an external Cascading Style Sheet.

Example (HTML)

```
<head>
<link rel="stylesheet" href="/pathname/stylesheet.css"
type="text/css">
</head>
```

Example (XHTML)

```
<head>
<link rel="stylesheet" href="/pathname/stylesheet.css"
type="text/css" />
</head>
```

---

map   HTML 4.01 | HTML5

```
<map> . . . </map>
```

Specifies a client-side image map. It contains some number of area elements that establish clickable regions within the image map.

Notes

The map must be named using the name attribute in HTML documents, the id attribute in XHTML documents, or both for backward compatibility. When both are used, they must have the same value.

---

map | 103

Start/End Tags

Required/Required

Attributes

Core, Internationalization, Events, HTML5 Global Attributes

id="*text*"
> **Required in XHTML**. Gives the map a unique name so that it can be referenced from a link, script, or style sheet.

name="*text*"
> **Required in HTML 4.01 and 5; deprecated in XHTML 1.0 only;** *use* id *instead*. Gives the image map a name that is then referenced within the img element.

Example

```
<map name="space" id="space">
  <area shape="rect" coords="203,23,285,106"
    href=http://www.nasa.gov alt="">
  <area shape="circle" coords="372,64,40"
    href="mypage.html" alt="">
</map>
```

---

mark   HTML5

<mark> . . . </mark>

Represents a selection of text that has been marked or highlighted for reference purposes or to bring it to the attention of the reader. Marked text is considered to be of particular relevance to the user.

Notes

HTML5 only.

Start/End Tags

Required/Required

Attributes

HTML5 Global Attributes

Example

In this example, a user's search query ("estate tax") is marked in the returned document:

```
<p> ... PART I. ADMINISTRATION OF THE GOVERNMENT. TITLE IX.
TAXATION. CHAPTER 65C. MASS. <mark>ESTATE TAX</mark>.
Chapter 65C: Sect. 2. Computation of <mark>estate
tax</mark>.</p>
```

---

menu   HTML 4.01 | HTML5

```
<menu> . . . </menu>
```

In HTML 4.01, the deprecated menu element indicates a menu list, which consists of one or more list items (li). Menus were intended for a list of short choices, such as a menu of links to other documents.

In HTML5, menu represents a list of interactive options or commands such as a menu of options in a web application.

Start/End Tags

Required/Required

Attributes

Core, Internationalization, Events, HTML5 Global Attributes

compact *(compact="compact" in XHTML)*
> **Deprecated. Not in HTML5**. Makes the list as small as possible. Few browsers support the compact attribute.

label="*text*"
> **HTML5 only**. Specifies a label for the menu, which can be displayed in nested menus.

type="context|toolbar"
> **HTML5 only**. Identifies the menu state. context indicates a context menu that can be accessed only when it is activated. toolbar indicates the menu is to be used as a toolbar that can be interacted with immediately. If the type attribute is omitted, the default is merely a list of commands.

Example (HTML 4.01)

```
<menu>
  <li>About</li>
  <li>News</li>
  <li>Blog</li>
  <li>Contact</li>
</menu>
```

Example (HTML5)

```
<menu>
  <command onclick="cut()" label="Cut">
  <command onclick="copy()" label="Copy">
  <command onclick="paste()" label="Paste">
  <command onclick="delete()" label="Clear">
</menu>
```

---

meta   HTML 4.01 | HTML5

HTML: <meta>; *XHTML:* <meta/> *or* <meta />

Provides additional information about the document. It should be placed within the head of the document. It is commonly used to identify its media type and character set. It can also provide keywords, author information, descriptions, and other metadata. The head element may contain more than one meta element.

Start/End Tags

This is an empty element. In HTML, the end tag is forbidden. In XHTML, the element must be closed with a trailing slash as just shown. Developers may include a space character before the slash for backward compatibility with older browsers.

Attributes

Internationalization, HTML5 Global Attributes

charset="*character set*"
> **HTML5 only**. Can be used with the meta element as a substitute for the http-equiv method for declaring the character set of the document.

`content="`*`text`*`"`

> ***Required***. Specifies the value of the meta element property and is always used in conjunction with `name` or `http-equiv`.

`http-equiv="`*`text`*`"`

> The specified information is treated as though it were included in the HTTP header that the server sends ahead of the document. It is used in conjunction with the `content` attribute (in place of the `name` attribute).

`id="`*`text`*`"`

> ***XHTML and HTML5***. Assigns a unique identifying name to the element.

`name="`*`text`*`"`

> Specifies a name for the `meta` information property.

`scheme="`*`text`*`"`

> ***Not in HTML5***. Provides additional information for the interpretation of metadata.

Example (HTML)

```
<meta name="copyright" content="2006, O'Reilly Media">
```

Examples (XHTML)

```
<meta http-equiv="content-type" content="text/html;
charset=UTF-8" />
<meta http-equiv="refresh" content= "15" />
```

Example (HTML5)

```
<meta charset="UTF-8">
```

---

meter   HTML5

`<meter> . . . </meter>`

Represents a fractional value or a scalar measurement within a known range (also known as a *gauge*). It should not be used to indicate progress (such as a progress bar) or when there is no known maximum value.

Notes

HTML5 only.

Start/End Tags

Required/Required

Attributes

HTML5 Global Attributes

high="*number*"
> Indicates the range that is considered to be "high" for the gauge

low="*number*"
> Indicates the range that is considered to be "low" for the gauge

max="*number*"
> Specifies the maximum or highest value of the range

min="*number*"
> Specifies the minimum or lowest value of the range

optimum="*number*"
> Indicates the range that is considered to be "optimum" for the gauge

value="*number*"
> Specifies the actual or "measured" value for the gauge

Examples

The following examples show three methods for indicating a measurement of 50%:

```
<meter>50%</meter>

<meter min="0" max="200">100</meter>

<meter min="0" max="200" value="100"></meter>
```

`<nav> . . . </nav>`

Represents a section of the document intended for navigation. Not all lists of links are appropriate for nav, only those that represent major navigation blocks on a page or within a section. The links within a nav element can be to other documents or to other areas within the current document.

Notes

HTML5 only.

Start/End Tags

Required/Required

Attributes

HTML5 Global Attributes

Example

```
<nav>
  <ul>
    <li><a href="">About us</a></li>
    <li><a href="">Contact</a></li>
    <li><a href="">Home</a></li>
  </ul>
</nav>
```

noembed

`<noembed> . . . </noembed>`

Nonstandard. The text or object in the noembed element appears when an embedded object cannot be displayed (such as when the appropriate plug-in is not available). This element is used within or after the embed element.

Notes

This element is not included in any HTML specification.

Start/End Tags

Not formally defined, but both are required in common use.

Attributes

None

Example

```
<embed src="movies/vacation.mov" width="240" height="196"
 pluginspage="http://www.apple.com/quicktime/download/">
   <noembed><img src="vacation.gif" alt="">You do not seem
to have the plugin.</noembed>
 </embed>
```

---

noframes   HTML 4.01

`<noframes>` . . . `</noframes>`

Defines content to be displayed by user agents (browsers) that cannot display frames. Browsers that do support frames ignore the content in the noframes element.

Notes

Not in HTML5. The frameset, frame, and noframes elements are not included in HTML5.

Start/End Tags

Required/Required

Attributes

Core, Internationalization, Events

Example

See frameset.

noscript

`<noscript> . . . </noscript>`

Provides alternate content when a script cannot be executed. The content of this element may be rendered if the user agent doesn't support scripting, if scripting support is turned off, or if the browser doesn't recognize the scripting language.

Notes

noscript is not included in the XML syntax of HTML5 because the element relies on an HTML parser. When noscript appears in the head of a document, it may only contain link, style, and meta elements.

Start/End Tags

Required/Required

Attributes

Core, Internationalization, Events, HTML5 Global Attributes

Example

```
<script type="text/JavaScript">
... script here
</script>
<noscript>
<p>This function requires JavaScript to be enabled.</p>
</noscript>
```

object

`<object> . . . </object>`

A generic element used for embedding media (such as an image, applet, movie, audio, or even another HTML file) on a web page. The attributes required for the object element vary with the type of content it is placing. The object element may contain content that will be rendered if the object cannot be embedded. The object element may also contain a number of param elements that pass important information to the object when it displays or plays. Not all objects require additional parameters. The object and param elements work together to allow authors to specify three types of information:

- The implementation of the object—that is, the executable code that runs in order to render the object.
- The data to be rendered. The **data** attribute specifies the location of the resource, in most cases an external file, such as a movie or a PDF file.
- Additional settings required by the object at runtime. Some embedded media objects require additional settings that get called into play when the object plays or is rendered.

Notes

The object element began as a proprietary element in Internet Explorer to support ActiveX and later Java applets. Browser support for the object element does not live up to the W3C's vision of object as an all-purpose object placer; for example, it is not currently possible to reliably place images with the object element.

Start/End Tags

Required/Required

Attributes

Core, Internationalization, Events, HTML5 Global Attributes

align="bottom|middle|top|left|right"
> ***Deprecated. Not in HTML5***. Aligns object with respect to surrounding text. See the img element for explanations of the align values.

archive="*URLs*"
> ***Not in HTML5***. Specifies a space-separated list of URLs for resources that are related to the object.

border="*number*"
> ***Deprecated. Not in HTML5***. Sets the width of the border in pixels if the object is a link.

---

classid="*URI*"

> ***Not in HTML5***. Identifies the location of an object's implementation. It is used with or in place of the `data` attribute. The syntax depends on the object type. Not supported by Gecko browsers.

codebase="*URI*"

> ***Not in HTML5***. Identifies the base URL used to resolve relative URLs in the object (similar to `base`). By default, `codebase` is the base URL of the current document.

codetype="*content-type*"

> ***Not in HTML5***. Specifies the media type of the code. It is required only if the browser cannot determine an applet's MIME type from the `classid` attribute or if the server does not deliver the correct MIME type when downloading the object.

data="*URI*"

> Specifies the address of the resource. The syntax depends on the object.

declare *(declare="declare" in XHTML)*

> ***Not in HTML5***. Declares an object but restrains the browser from downloading and processing it. Used in conjunction with the `name` attribute, this facility is similar to a forward declaration in a more conventional programming language, letting you defer the download until the object actually gets used.

form="*form id*"

> ***HTML5 only***. Associates the `object` with a `form` element on the page.

height="*number*"

> Specifies the height of the object in pixels.

hspace="*number*"

> ***Deprecated. Not in HTML5***. Specifies the number of pixels of clear space to the left and right of the object.

name="*text*"

> Specifies the name of the object to be referenced by scripts on the page.

standby="*message*"

> ***Not in HTML5***. Specifies the message to display during object loading.

tabindex="*number*"

> Specifies the position of the current element in the tabbing order for the current document. The value must be between 0 and 32,767. It is used for tabbing through the links on a page (or fields in a form).

type="*type*"

> Specifies the media type of the resource.

usemap="*URL*"

> Specifies the image map to use with the object.

vspace="*number*"

> ***Deprecated. Not in HTML5***. Specifies the number of pixels of clear space above and below the object.

width="*number*"

> Specifies the object width in pixels.

Example

```
<object classid="clsid:6BF52A52-394A-11d3-B153-00C04F79FAA6"
height="280" width="320"
codebase="http://activex.microsoft.com/activex/controls/
mplayer/en/nsmp2inf.cab#version=6,4,7,111">
    <param name="URL" value="movies/europe.wmv">
    <param name="autoStart" value="false">
    <param name="UIMode" value="full">
You do not have Windows Media Player installed.
Get it here.
</object>
```

---

ol

HTML 4.01 | HTML5

<ol> . . . </ol>

Defines an ordered (numbered) list that consists of one or more list items (li). The user agent inserts item numbers automatically.

Start/End Tags

Required/Required

Attributes

Core, Internationalization, Events, HTML5 Global Attributes

compact *(compact="compact" in XHTML)*
> **Deprecated. Not in HTML5**. Displays the list as small as possible. Few browsers support the compact attribute.

reversed *(reversed="reversed" in XHTML)*
> **HTML5 only**. Reverses the numbering sequence, from highest to lowest value.

start="*number*"
> **Deprecated. Included in HTML5**. Starts the numbering of the list at *number* instead of at 1.

type="1|A|a|I|i"
> **Deprecated. Not in HTML5**. Defines the numbering system for the list as follows:

Type value	Generated style	Sample sequence
1	Arabic numerals (default)	1, 2, 3, 4
A	Uppercase letters	A, B, C, D
a	Lowercase letters	a, b, c, d
I	Uppercase Roman numerals	I, II, III, IV
i	Lowercase Roman numerals	i, ii, iii, iv

Example

```
<ol>
  <li>Get out of bed</li>
  <li>Take a shower</li>
  <li>Walk the dog</li>
</ol>
```

optgroup   HTML 4.01 | HTML5

<optgroup> . . . </optgroup>

Defines a logical group of option elements within a select menu form control. An optgroup element may not contain other optgroup elements (they may not be nested).

Start/End Tags

HTML 4.01 and XHTML: Required/Required;
HTML5: Required/Optional

Attributes

Core, Internationalization, Events, HTML5 Global Attributes

disabled *(disabled="disabled" in XHTML)*
> Indicates that the group of options is nonfunctional. It can be reactivated with a script.

label="text"
> **Required**. Specifies the label for the option group.

Example

```
<p>What are your favorite ice cream flavors?<p>
<select name="ice_cream" size="6" multiple="multiple">
<optgroup label="traditional">
   <option>Vanilla</option>
   <option>Chocolate</option>
</optgroup>
<optgroup label="specialty">
   <option>Inside-out Rocky Road</option>
   <option>Super-duper Praline Pecan Smashup</option>
</optgroup>
</select>
```

---

option   HTML 4.01 | HTML5

<option> . . . </option>

Defines an option within a select element (a multiple-choice menu or scrolling list). The content of the option element is the value that is sent to the form-processing application (unless an alternative value is specified using the value attribute).

Note

In HTML5, the option element may also be used within the new datalist element.

Start/End Tags

HTML: Required/Optional; XHTML: Required/Required

Attributes

Core, Internationalization, Events, HTML5 Global Attributes

disabled (disabled="disabled" *in XHTML*)
> Indicates that the selection is initially nonfunctional. It can be reactivated with a script.

label="*text*"
> Allows the author to provide a shorter label than the content of the option. This attribute is not supported.

selected (selected="selected" *in XHTML*)
> Makes this item selected when the form is initially displayed.

value="*text*"
> Defines a value to assign to the option item within the select control to use in place of option contents.

Example

```
<p>What are your favorite ice cream flavors?</p>
<select name="ice_cream" size="4" multiple="multiple">
   <option>Vanilla</option>
   <option>Chocolate</option>
   <option>Inside-out Rocky Road</option>
   <option>Super-duper Praline Pecan Smashup</option>
   <option>Mint Chocolate Chip</option>
   <option>Pistachio</option>
</select>
```

output   HTML5

. . .

Represents the result of a calculation, most likely the output of a script.

Notes

HTML5 only.

Start/End Tags

Required/Required

Attributes

HTML5 Global Attributes

for="*text*"
> Creates an explicit relationship between the calculation result and a named element or elements on the page.

form="*id of form owner*"
> Explicitly associates the input control with its associated form (its *form owner*). With this method, the input control does not need to be a child of the applicable form element.

name="*text*"
> Give an identifying name to the element.

Example

```
Total: <output name="total" onformchange="value =
round1.value + round2.value">0</output>
```

---

p HTML 4.01 | HTML5

`<p> . . . </p>`

Denotes a paragraph. Paragraphs may contain text and inline elements, but they may not contain other block elements, including other paragraphs. Browsers are instructed to ignore multiple empty p elements.

Start/End Tags

HTML: Required/Optional; XHTML: Required/Required

Attributes

Core, Internationalization, Events, HTML5 Global Attributes

align="center|left|right"
> **Deprecated. Not in HTML5**. Aligns the text within the element to the left, right, or center of the page.

Example

```
<p> Paragraphs are the most rudimentary elements of a text
document.</p>
<p>They are indicated by the <code>p</code> element.</p>
```

---

param

HTML: `<param>`; *XHTML:* `<param/>` *or* `<param />`

Supplies a parameter within an `applet` or `object` element. A parameter is info required by the applet or media object at runtime.

Start/End Tags

This is an empty element. In HTML, the end tag is forbidden. In XHTML, the element must be closed with a trailing slash as just shown. Developers may include a space character before the slash for backward compatibility with older browsers.

Attributes

HTML5 Global Attributes

`id="text"`
> Provides a name (similar to the `name` attribute) so that it can be referenced from a link, script, or style sheet.

`name="text"`
> **Required**. Defines the name of the parameter.

`type="content type"`
> **Not in HTML5**. Specifies the media type of the resource only when the `valuetype` attribute is set to `ref`. It describes the types of values found at the referred location.

`value="text"`
> Defines the value of the parameter.

`valuetype="data|ref|object"`
> **Not in HTML5**. Indicates the type of value: `data` indicates that the parameter's value is data (default); `ref` indicates that the parameter's value is a URL; `object` indicates that the value is the URL of another object in the document.

Example (HTML)

```
<param name="autoStart" value="false">
```

Example (XHTML)

```
<param name="autoStart" value="false" />
```

See object for additional examples.

---

pre <inline_reference/> HTML 4.01 | HTML5

`<pre> . . . </pre>`

Delimits "preformatted" text, meaning that lines are displayed exactly as they are typed in, honoring whitespace such as multiple character spaces and line breaks. By default, text within a pre element is displayed in a monospace font such as Courier. The example below would be rendered about the same in the browser as it appears in this book.

Start/End Tags

Required/Required

Attributes

Core, Internationalization, Events, HTML5 Global Attributes

`width="`*number*`"`
> **Deprecated. Not in HTML5.** This optional attribute determines how many characters to fit on a single line within the pre block.

`xml:space="preserve"`
> **XHTML only.** Instructs XML processors to preserve the whitespace in the element.

Example

```
<pre>
This is                 an              example of

        text with a         lot of
                            curious
                            whitespace.
</pre>
```

progress

`<progress> . . . </progress>`

Represents the completion progress of a task, such as downloading. The value measuring task completion can be provided by a script and inserted as content of the progress element or be provided with the value attribute. The progress element may be used even if the maximum value is not known, for example, to indicate a task waiting for a remote host to respond.

Notes

HTML5 only.

Start/End Tags

Required/Required

Attributes

HTML5 Global Attributes

`max="`*number*`"`

> Indicates a measure of the total work the task requires. The default is 1.

`value="`*number*`"`

> Specifies how much of the task has been completed.

Example

```
<p>Percent downloaded: <progress max="100"><span
id="completed">0</span>%</progress></p>
```

---

q   HTML 4.01

`<q> . . . </q>`

Delimits a short quotation that can be included inline, such as "to be or not to be." It differs from blockquote, which is a block-level element used for longer quotations. According to the specification, the user agent should automatically insert quotation marks before and after a quote element (however, Internet Explorer versions 7 and earlier do not support this feature). When used with the lang (language) attribute, the browser may insert language-specific quotation marks.

Start/End Tags

Required/Required

Attributes

Core, Internationalization, Events, HTML5 Global Attributes

cite="*URL*"
> Designates the source document from which the quotation was taken.

Example

```
<p>In that famous speech beginning, <q>Four score and
seven years ago,</q> ... </p>
```

---

rp

HTML5

`<rp> . . . </rp>`

Used within the ruby element to provide parentheses around ruby text to be shown by user agents that don't support ruby annotations.

Notes

HTML5 only.

Start/End Tags

Required/Required

Attributes

HTML5 Global Attributes

Example

See also the ruby listing.

In the following example, a browser that cannot display ruby annotation would display the rt content in parentheses after the ideograph:

```
<ruby>
汉 <rp>(</rp><rt>hàn</rt><rp>)</rp>
字 <rp>(</rp><rt>zì</rt><rp>)</rp>
</ruby>
```

This example was taken from the HTML5 Working Draft at whatwg.com, used with permission under an MIT License.

---

rt

`<rt> . . . </rt>`

Used within the ruby element, rt provides the ruby text in ruby annotations. The hints typically render smaller nearby the original ideograph.

Notes

HTML5 only.

Start/End Tags

Required/Required

Attributes

HTML5 Global Attributes

Example

See the ruby listing example.

---

ruby

`<ruby> . . . </ruby>`

Represents a run of text marked with *ruby annotations*, short guides to pronunciation, and other notes used primarily in East Asian typography.

Notes

HTML5 only.

Start/End Tags

Required/Required

Attributes

HTML5 Global Attributes

Example

In the following example, the pronunciation tips in the rt elements will be displayed above the ideographs in visual browsers:

```
<ruby>
汉 <rt>hàn</rt>
字 <rt>zì</rt>
</ruby>
```

This example was taken from the HTML5 Working Draft at whatwg.com, used with permission under an MIT License.

---

s   **HTML 4.01**

`<s> . . . </s>`

Enclosed text is displayed as strikethrough text (same as strike but introduced by later browser versions). Developers are advised to use style sheets to create strikethrough text instead of the s element.

Notes

Deprecated in HTML 4.01/XHTML 1.0. ***Not in HTML5***.

Start/End Tags

Required/Required

Attributes

Core, Internationalization, Events

Example

```
<p>All winter gear is <s>20%</s> 40% off.</p>
```

---

samp

`<samp> . . . </samp>`

Indicates sample output from programs, scripts, and so on.

Start/End Tags

Required/Required

Attributes

Core, Internationalization, Events, HTML5 Global Attributes

Example

```
<p>Provide alternative error messages to <samp>404 Not
Found</samp>.</p>
```

---

script

`<script> . . . </script>`

Places a script in the document (usually JavaScript for web documents). It may appear any number of times in the head or body of the document. The script may be provided in the script element or in an external file (by providing the src attribute).

Notes

In XHTML, when the script is provided as the content of the script element (i.e., not as an external file), the script should be contained in a CDATA section as shown in the example below.

Start/End Tags

Required/Required

Attributes

HTML5 Global Attributes

async *(async="async" in XHTML5)*
> **HTML5 only**. Indicates the script should be executed asynchronously, as soon as it is available.

`charset="`*`character set`*`"`

>Indicates the character encoding of an external script document (it is not relevant to the content of the script element).

`defer` *(defer="defer" in XHTML)*

>Indicates to the user agent that the script should be executed when the page is finished parsing.

`id="`*`text`*`"`

>**XHTML and HTML5**. Assigns a unique identifying name to the element.

`language="`*`text`*`"`

>**Deprecated**. Provides the name of the scripting language, but since it is not standardized, it has been deprecated in favor of the type attribute.

`src="`*`URL`*`"`

>Provides the location of an external script.

`type="`*`content-type`*`"`

>**Required in HTML 4.01. Optional in HTML5 if using JavaScript**. Specifies the scripting language used for the current script. This setting overrides any default script setting for the document. The value is a content type, most often text/javascript.

`xml:space="preserve"`

>**XHTML only**. Instructs XML processors to preserve the whitespace in the element.

Example (HTML 4.01 and XHTML 1.0)

```
<script type="text/javascript">
  // <![CDATA[
  . . . JavaScript code goes here . . .
  // ]]>
</script>
```

Example (HTML5)

```
<script>
// <![CDATA[
  . . . JavaScript code goes here . . .
  // ]]>
</script>
```

---

section

`<section> . . . </section>`

Represents a section (a thematic grouping of content) of a document or application with its own internal outline and (optionally) a header and footer. The section element is not a generic container; it should be used only if the element's contents should appear in the document's outline.

Notes

HTML5 only.

Start/End Tags

Required/Required

Attributes

HTML5 Global Attributes

`cite="text"`

   Provides a link to information about the source or author of the section.

Example

```
<body>
<article>
<h1>Common Birds</h1>
<section>
  <h1>Chapter 1: Hummingbirds</h1>
  <p>A little something on hummingbirds.</p>
</section>
<section>
  <h1>Chapter 2: Turkeys</h1>
  <p>This is about turkeys</p>
</section>
 </article>
</body>
```

`<select> . . . </select>`

Defines a multiple-choice menu or a scrolling list. It is a container for one or more `option` or `optgroup` elements.

Start/End Tags

Required/Required

Attributes

Core, Internationalization, Events; plus onfocus, onblur, onchange, *HTML5 Global Attributes*

autofocus *(autofocus="autofocus" in XHTML)*
> ***HTML5 only***. Indicates the control should have focus (be highlighted and ready for user input) when the document loads.

disabled *(disabled="disabled" in XHTML)*
> Indicates that the select element is initially nonfunctional. It can be reactivated with a script.

form="*id of the form owner*"
> ***HTML5 only***. Explicitly associates the input control with its associated form (its *form owner*). With this method, the input control does not need to be a child of the form element that applies to it.

multiple *(multiple="multiple" in XHTML)*
> Allows the user to select more than one option from the list. When this attribute is absent, only single selections are allowed.

name="*text*"
> ***Required***. Defines the name for the select control. When the form is submitted to the form-processing application, this name is sent along with each selected option value.

size="*number*"
> Specifies the number of rows that display in the list of options. For values higher than 1, the options are displayed as a scrolling list with the specified number of options visible. When size="1" is specified, the list is displayed as a pop-up menu.

The default value is 1 when `multiple` is *not* used. When `multiple` is specified, the value varies by browser (but a value of 4 is common).

tabindex="*number*"

Specifies position in the tabbing order. Tabbing navigation allows the user to cycle through the active fields by using the Tab key.

Example

```
<p>What are your favorite ice cream flavors?</p>
<select name="ice_cream" multiple="multiple">
   <option>Vanilla</option>
   <option>Chocolate</option>
   <option>Mint Chocolate Chip</option>
   <option>Pistachio</option>
</select>
```

---

small   HTML 4.01 | HTML5

`<small> . . . </small>`

Renders the type smaller than the surrounding text. Use of this element should be avoided in favor of style sheets for controlling font size.

Notes

This element has been redefined in HTML5 to represent "small print" (e.g., for legal notes).

Start/End Tags

Required/Required

Attributes

Core, Internationalization, Events, HTML5 Global Attributes

Example

```
<p><small>Copyright 2010, O'Reilly Media</small></p>
```

HTML: `<source>`; *XHTML:* `<source/>` *or* `<source />`

Used within `audio` and `video` elements, `source` allows authors to specify multiple versions of a media file. When source is used, the `src` attribute should be omitted from the `audio` and `video` elements. User agents will go down the list of `source` elements until they find a format they are able to play.

Notes

HTML5 only.

Start/End Tags

This is an empty element. It must be closed with a trailing slash in XHTML5.

Attributes

HTML5 Global Attributes

`media="all|aural|braille|handheld|print|projection|screen|tty|tv"`

> Specifies the target display media for the audio or video file.

`src="URL"`

> Specifies the location of the audio or video file.

`type="MIME type"`

> Indicates the file type of the media file and may also include the `codecs=` MIME parameter indicating the codec used to encode the media.

Example

```
<video>
  <source src="media/vacation.ogv" type="video/ogg;
  codecs='theora, vorbis'">
  <source src="media/vacation.mp4" type="video/mp4">
  Your browser doesn't support the <code>video</code>
  element.
</video>
```

span

`<span> . . . </span>`

Identifies a generic inline element. The span element is typically given meaning with the class or id attributes, which also allow it to be accessible to scripts and selected in style sheets.

Start/End Tags

Required/Required

Attributes

Core, Internationalization, Events, HTML5 Global Attributes

Example

```
Jenny: <span class="tel">867.5309</span>
```

strike

`<strike> . . . </strike>`

Displays enclosed text as strikethrough text (crossed through with a horizontal line). It has been deprecated in HTML 4.01 and removed in HTML5 in favor of style sheet controls.

Notes

Deprecated in HTML 4.01/XHTML. ***Not in HTML5***.

Start/End Tags

Required/Required

Attributes

Core, Internationalization, Events

Example

```
That is a <strike>seperate</strike> separate issue.
```

strong HTML 4.01 | HTML5

`<strong>` . . . `</strong>`

Enclosed text is strongly emphasized.

Notes

In HTML5, strong has been slightly redefined as denoting importance, not strong emphasis.

Start/End Tags

Required/Required

Attributes

Core, Internationalization, Events, HTML5 Global Attributes

Example

    Get yours ****while supplies last!****

---

style HTML 4.01 | HTML5

`<style>` . . . `</style>`

Inserts style information (commonly Cascading Style Sheets) into the head of a document.

Notes

In HTML5, the style element may be used in the content of the document.

Start/End Tags

Required/Required

Attributes

Internationalization, HTML5 Global Attributes

id="*text*"
> ***XHTML and XHTML5***. Assigns a unique identifying name to the element.

---

132 | HTML and XHTML Pocket Reference

```
media="all|aural|braille|handheld|print|projection|screen|
tty|tv"
```
> Specifies the intended destination medium for the style infor-
> mation. It may be a single keyword or a comma-separated list.
> The default in the HTML 4.01 spec is screen. In HTML5, the
> default is all.

scoped *(scoped="scoped" in XHTML5)*
> **HTML5 only**. Applies the styles only to the local document
> tree (i.e., only the descendants of the parent of the style
> element).

title="*text*"
> Gives the embedded style sheet a title.

type="*content type*" *(text/css)*
> **Required in HTML 4.01**. Specifies the style sheet language.
> For Cascading Style Sheets (currently the only style type
> option), the value is text/css. In HTML5, the type attribute
> is optional if using CSS.

xml:space="preserve"
> **XHTML only**. Instructs XML processors to preserve the
> whitespace in the element.

Example

Note that the type attribute is optional in HTML5 when using CSS.

```
<head>
<style type="text/css">
   h1 {color: #666;}
</style>
<title>Scientific Presentation</title>
</head>
```

---

sub

```
<sub> . . . </sub>
```

Formats enclosed text as subscript.

Start/End Tags

Required/Required

Attributes

Core, Internationalization, Events, HTML5 Global Attributes

Example

```
<p>H<sub>2</sub>0</p>
```

---

sup   HTML 4.01 | HTML5

```
<sup> . . . </sup>
```

Formats enclosed text as superscript.

Start/End Tags

Required/Required

Attributes

Core, Internationalization, Events, HTML5 Global Attributes

Example

```
<p>E=MC<sup>2</sup></p>
```

---

table   HTML 4.01 | HTML5

```
<table> . . . </table>
```

Indicates a table used for displaying rows and columns of data or information. The minimum elements for defining a table are table for establishing the table itself, tr for declaring a table row, and td for creating table cells within the row. The complete table model is shown below.

Start/End Tags

Required/Required

Attributes

Core, Internationalization, Events, HTML5 Global Attributes

`align="left|right|center"`

> **Deprecated. Not in HTML5**. Aligns the table within the text flow (same as `align` in the `img` element). The default alignment is `left`. The `center` value is not universally supported.

`bgcolor="#rrggbb"` *or* `"color name"`

> **Deprecated. Not in HTML5**. Specifies a background color for the entire table. The color is specified in hexadecimal RGB values or by color name. Style sheets are the proper way to specify colors.

`border="number"`

> **Not in HTML5**. Specifies the width (in pixels) of the border around the table and its cells. Setting its value to 0 (zero) turns the borders off completely. The default value is 1. Adding the word `border` without a value results in a 1-pixel border, although this is not valid in XHTML.

`cellpadding="number"`

> **Not in HTML5**. Sets the amount of space, in number of pixels, between the cell border and its contents. The default value is 1.

`cellspacing="number"`

> **Not in HTML5**. Sets the amount of space (in number of pixels) between table cells. The default value is 2.

`frame="void|above|below|hsides|lhs|rhs|vsides|box|border"`

> **Not in HTML5**. Tells the browser where to draw borders around the table. The values are:

Value	Description
void	The frame does not appear (default).
above	Top side only.
below	Bottom side only.
hsides	Top and bottom sides only.
vsides	Right and left sides only.
lhs	Left side only.
rhs	Right side only.
box	All four sides.
border	All four sides.

table | 135

height="*number*" or "*percentage*"

Nonstandard. Specifies the minimum height of the entire table. It can be specified in a specific number of pixels or by a percentage of the parent element. Because this attribute is nonstandard, using it will cause a document to not validate.

rules="all|cols|groups|none|rows"

Not in HTML5. Tells the browser where to draw rules within the table. When the border attribute is set to a value greater than zero, rules defaults to all unless otherwise specified. This attribute is not universally supported. Its values are:

Value	Description
all	Rules appear between all rows and columns.
cols	Rules appear between columns only.
groups	Rules appear between row groups (thead, tfoot, and tbody) and column groups.
none	No rules (default).
rows	Rules appear between rows only.

summary="*text*"

Provides a summary of the table contents for use with nonvisual browsers. In HTML5, authors are urged to use the caption element instead.

width="*number*" or "*percentage*"

Not in HTML5. Specifies the width of the entire table. It can be specified by number of pixels or by percentage of the parent element.

Examples

A simple table with two rows and two columns.

```
<table width="70%" cellpadding="10">
<tr>
    <td>cell 1</td><td>cell 2</td>
</tr>
<tr>
    <td>cell 3</td><td>cell 4</td>
</tr>
</table>
```

The proper element order in the full table model (shown in HTML syntax). For details, see the caption, tbody, thead, tfoot, colgroup, and col element entries.

```
<table>
<caption>Employee salaries and start dates</caption>

<colgroup id=" employeeinfo">
    <col span="2" width="300">
    <col span="1" width="100" class="date">
</colgroup>

<thead>
<tr>
<th>Employee</th><th>Salary</th><th>Start date</th>
</tr>
</thead>

<tfoot>
<tr><td colspan="3">Compiled by Betty D. Boss</td></tr>
</tfoot>


<tbody>
<tr>
<td>Wilma</td><td>50,000</td><td>April 6</td>
</tr>
<tr>...more data cells...</tr>
<tr>...more data cells...</tr>
</tbody>

</table>
```

tbody   HTML 4.01 | HTML5

`<tbody> . . . </tbody>`

Defines a row or group of rows as the "body" of the table. It must contain at least one row element (tr). "Row group" elements (tbody, thead, and tfoot) could speed table display and provide a mechanism for scrolling the body of a table independently of its head and foot. Row groups could also be useful for printing long tables for which the head information could be printed on each page. The char and charoff attributes are not well supported.

Start/End Tags

HTML: Optional/Optional; XHTML: Required/Required

Attributes

Core, Internationalization, Events, HTML5 Global Attributes

`align="left|right|center|justify|char"`

> **Not in HTML5**. Specifies the horizontal alignment of text in a cell or cells. The default value is `left`. The `align` attribute as it applies to table cell content was not deprecated in HTML 4.01/XHTML but has been removed from HTML5 in favor of style sheet controls.

`char="character"`

> **Not in HTML5**. Specifies a character along which the cell contents will be aligned when `align` is set to `char`. The default character is a decimal point (language-appropriate). This attribute is generally not supported.

`charoff="length"`

> **Not in HTML5**. Specifies the offset distance to the first alignment character on each line. This attribute is generally not supported.

`valign="top|middle|bottom|baseline"`

> **Not in HTML5**. Specifies the vertical alignment of text in the cells of a column.

Example

See `table`.

---

td HTML 4.01 | HTML5

`<td>` . . . `</td>`

Defines a table data cell. A table cell may contain any content, including another table.

Start/End Tags

HTML: Required/Optional; XHTML: Required/Required

Attributes

Core, Internationalization, Events, HTML5 Global Attributes

abbr="*text*"
> **Not in HTML5**. Provides an abbreviated form of the cell's content.

align="left|right|center|justify|char"
> **Not in HTML5**. Specifies the horizontal alignment of text in a cell or cells. The default value is left.

axis="*text*"
> **Not in HTML5**. Places a cell into a conceptual category, which could then be used to organize or search the table in different ways.

background="*URL*"
> **Nonstandard**. Specifies a graphic image to be used as a tile within the cell. Style sheets should be used to position images in the background of table cells.

bgcolor="*#rrggbb*" or "*color name*"
> **Deprecated. Not in HTML5**. Specifies a color to be used in the table cell. A cell's background color overrides colors specified at the row or table levels.

char="*character*"
> **Not in HTML5**. Specifies a character along which the cell contents will be aligned when align is set to char. The default character is a decimal point (language-appropriate). This attribute is generally not supported by current browsers.

charoff="*length*"
> **Not in HTML5**. Specifies the offset distance to the first alignment character on each line. If a line doesn't use an alignment character, it should be horizontally shifted to end at the alignment position. This attribute is generally not supported by current browsers.

colspan="*number*"
> Specifies the number of columns the current cell should span. The default value is 1. According to the HTML 4.01 specification, the value 0 (zero) means the current cell spans all columns from the current column to the last column in the table;

in reality, however, this feature is not supported in current browsers.

`headers="`*`id reference`*`"`
> Lists header cells (by `id`) that provide header information for the current data cell. This is intended to make tables more accessible to nonvisual browsers.

`height="`*`pixels`*`" or "`*`percentage`*`"`
> ***Deprecated. Not in HTML5***. Specifies the height of the cell in number of pixels or by a percentage value relative to the table height. The height specified in the first column will apply to the rest of the cells in the row. The height values need to be consistent for the cells in a particular row. Pixel measurements are more reliable than percentages, which work only when the height of the table is specified in pixels.

`nowrap` (`nowrap="nowrap"` in XHTML)
> ***Deprecated. Not in HTML5***. Disables automatic text wrapping for the current cell. Line breaks must be added with a `br` element or by starting a new paragraph.

`rowspan="`*`number`*`"`
> Specifies the number of rows spanned by the current cell. The default value is 1. According to the HTML 4.01 Recommendation, the value 0 (zero) means the current cell spans all rows from the current row to the last row; in reality, however, this feature is not supported by browsers.

`scope="row|col|rowgroup|colgroup"`
> ***Not in HTML5 for*** td. Specifies the table cells for which the current cell provides header information. A value of `col` indicates that the current cell is the header for all the cells that fall below. `colgroup` indicates the current cell is the header for the column group that contains it. A value of `row` means that the current cell is the header for the cells in the rest of the row. A value of `rowgroup` means the current cell is the header for the containing row group. This is intended to make tables more accessible to nonvisual browsers. ***NOTE***: *In HTML5, scope applies to the* th *element only*.

`valign="top|middle|bottom|baseline"`
> ***Not in HTML5***. Specifies the vertical alignment of text in the cells of a column.

```
width="pixels" or "percentage"
```
> **Deprecated. Not in HTML5**. Specifies the width of the cell
> in number of pixels or by a percentage value relative to the
> table width. The width specified in the first row will apply to
> the rest of the cells in the column, and the values need to be
> consistent for cells in the column.

Example

```
<table>
<tr>
   <td colspan="2">Cell 1</td>
</tr>
<tr>
   <td>Cell 3</td><td>Cell 4</td>
</tr>
</table>
```

textarea

```
<textarea> . . . </textarea>
```

Defines a multiline text entry control. The content of the `textarea`
element is displayed in the text entry field when the form initially
displays.

Start/End Tags
Required/Required

Attributes

Core, *Internationalization*, *Events*, *Focus*, onselect, onchange,
HTML5 Global Attributes

```
autofocus (autofocus="autofocus" in XHTML)
```
> **HTML5 only**. Indicates the control should have focus (be
> highlighted and ready for user input) when the document
> loads.

```
cols="number"
```
> **Required**. Specifies the visible width of the text entry field,
> measured in number of characters. Users may enter text lines
> that are longer than the provided width, in which case the entry

scrolls to the right (or wraps if the browser provides some mechanism for doing so).

`disabled` *(disabled="disabled" in XHTML)*

> Disables the control for user input. It can be altered only via a script. Browsers may display disabled controls differently (grayed out, for example), which could be useful for dimming certain controls until required info is supplied.

`form="id of form owner"`

> **HTML5 only**. Explicitly associates the input control with its associated form (its *form owner*). With this method, the input control does not need to be a child of the `form` element that applies to it.

`maxlength="number"`

> **HTML5 only**. Specifies the maximum number of characters the user can input for a text or password input element.

`name="text"`

> **Required**. Specifies a name for the text input control. This name will be sent along with the control content to the form-processing application.

`placeholder="number"`

> **HTML5 only**. Provides a short (one word or short phrase) hint or example to help the user enter the correct data. If a longer description is necessary, use the `title` attribute.

`readonly` *(readonly="readonly" in XHTML)*

> Indicates that the form control may not be modified.

`required` *(required="required" in XHTML)*

> **HTML5 only**. When present, indicates the input data is required.

`rows="number"`

> **Required**. Specifies the height of the text entry field in number of lines of text. If the user enters more lines than are visible, the text field scrolls down to accommodate the extra lines.

`wrap="hard|soft"`

> **HTML5 only**. When set to `hard`, hard returns (carriage return + line feed characters) are inserted at the end of lines as they appear in text entry field. When set to `hard`, there must also be

a cols attribute specifying the length of the line. When set to soft (the default), line breaks in the text entry field are not preserved in the returned data.

Example

```
<p>What did you dream last night?</p>
<textarea name="dream" rows="4" cols="45">Tell us your
    dream in 100 words or fewer.</textarea>
```

---

tfoot   HTML 4.01 | HTML5

`<tfoot> . . . </tfoot>`

Defines a table footer. It is one of the "row group" elements. The tfoot element must appear before the tbody within the table element. A tfoot element must contain at least one row (tr). See tbody listing for more information.

Start/End Tags

HTML 4.01: Required/Optional; XHTML: Required/Required; HTML5: Optional/Optional

Attributes

Same as tbody.

Example

See table.

---

th   HTML 4.01 | HTML5

`<th> . . . </th>`

Defines a table header cell. Table header cells provide important information and context to the table cells in the row or column that they precede. They are an important tool for making the information in tables accessible. In terms of markup, they function the same as table data cells (td).

Start/End Tags

HTML: Required/Optional; XHTML: Required/Required

Attributes

The th element accepts the same attributes as the td element. See listing under td.

Example

```
<table>
<tr><th>Planet</th><th>Distance from Earth</th></tr>
<tr><td>Venus</td><td>pretty darn far</td></tr>
<tr><td>Neptune</td><td>ridiculously far</td></tr>
</table>
```

thead   HTML 4.01 | HTML5

`<thead> . . . </thead>`

Defines the head of the table. The thead element is one of the "row group" elements. It may be used to duplicate headers when the full table is broken over pages or for a static header that appears with a scrolling table body. It must contain at least one row (tr).

Notes

In HTML5, the thead element may not contain td elements.

Start/End Tags

HTML 4.01: Required/Optional; XHTML: Required/Required; HTML5: Optional/Optional

Attributes

Same as tbody.

Example

See table.

```
<time> . . . </time>
```

Represents a time on a 24-hour clock or a date and/or a date on the Gregorian calendar. The time element could be used to pass time and date information in a machine-readable manner to other applications (e.g., saving an event to a personal calendar), or to restyle time information into alternate formats (e.g., 18:00 to 6 p.m.). The time element is not intended to be used to mark up times for which a precise time or date cannot be established, such as "the end of last year" or "the turn of the century."

Notes

HTML5 only.

Start/End Tags

Required/Required

Attributes

HTML5 Global Attributes

pubdate (pubdate="pubdate" *in XHTML*)

> Indicates that the date and time provided by datetime is the publication date and time of the parent element (the article or whole document).

datetime="*YYYY-MM-DDThh:mm:ssTZD*"

> Identifies the date or time being specified. If the datetime attribute is used, the time element may be empty.

Examples

```
The deadline for entries is <time datetime="2010-09-01T
20:00-05:00">September 1, 2010, 8pm EST</time>

Hours: <time>8am</time> to <time>9pm</time>
```

`<title> . . . </title>`

Required. Specifies the title of the document. All documents must contain a meaningful `title` within the head of the document. Titles should contain only ASCII characters (letters, numbers, and basic punctuation). Special characters (such as &) should be referred to by their character entities within the title.

There may be no more than one `title` element and it may not contain other elements.

Titles should be clear and descriptive. The title is typically displayed in the top bar of the browser, outside the regular content window, as well as in a user's bookmarks or favorites list. Search engines also rely heavily on document titles.

Start/End Tags

Required/Required

Attributes

Internationalization, HTML5 Global Attributes

`id="text"`
> ***XHTML and HTML5***. Assigns a unique identifying name to the element.

Example

```
<head>
<title>The Adventures of Peto &amp; Fleck</title>
</head>
```

`<tr> . . . </tr>`

Defines a row of cells within a table. A `tr` element may contain only some number of `td` and/or `th` elements. It may be used only within a `table`, `thead`, `tfoot`, or `tbody` element. Settings made in the `tr` element apply to all the cells in that row, however, the documented attributes below should be avoided in favor of style sheet controls.

Start/End Tags

HTML: Required/Optional; XHTML: Required/Required

Attributes

Core, Internationalization, Events, HTML5 Global Attributes

align="left|right|center|justify|char"
> **Not in HTML5**. Specifies the horizontal alignment of text in a cell or cells. The default value is left.

bgcolor="#rrggbb" *or* "color name"
> **Deprecated. Not in HTML5**. Specifies a background color to be used in the row. A row's background color overrides the color specified at the table level.

char="character"
> **Not in HTML5**. Specifies a character along which the cell contents will be aligned when align is set to char. The default character is a decimal point (language-appropriate). This attribute is generally not supported.

charoff="length"
> **Not in HTML5**. Specifies the offset distance to the first alignment character on each line. If a line doesn't use an alignment character, it should be horizontally shifted to end at the alignment position. This attribute is generally not supported by current browsers.

valign="top|middle|bottom|baseline"
> **Not in HTML5**. Specifies the vertical alignment of text in the cells of a column.

Example

```
<table>
<tr>
    <td>cell 1</td><td>cell 2</td>
</tr>
<tr>
    <td>cell 3</td><td>cell 4</td>
</tr>
</table>
```

tt

`<tt> . . . </tt>`

Formats enclosed text as teletype or monospaced text.

Notes

Not in HTML5.

Start/End Tags

Required/Required

Attributes

Core, *Internationalization*, *Events*

Example

```
<p>Enter your birthday (Ex: <tt>07.19.1975</tt>):</p>
```

---

u

`<u> . . . </u>`

Enclosed text is underlined when displayed. Underlined text may be confused as a hypertext link, but if underlining is required, Cascading Style Sheets is the preferred method.

Notes

Deprecated in HTML 4.01/XHTML 1.0. *Not in HTML5*.

Attributes

Core, *Internationalization*, *Events*

Example

```
<p><u>Underlined text</u> may be mistaken for a link.</p>
```

`<ul> . . . </ul>`

Defines an unordered list, in which list items (`li`) have no sequence. By default, browsers insert bullets before each item in an unordered list. Lists may be formatted in any fashion (including as horizontal navigation elements) using Cascading Style Sheet properties.

Start/End Tags

Required/Required

Attributes

Core, Internationalization, Events, HTML5 Global Attributes

`compact="compact"`
> ***Deprecated. Not in HTML5***. Displays the list block as small as possible. Few browsers support this attribute.

`type="disc|circle|square"`
> ***Deprecated. Not in HTML5***. Defines the shape of the bullets used for each list item.

Example

```
<ul>
    <li>About</li>
    <li>Portfolio</li>
    <li>Blog</li>
    <li>Contact</li>
</ul>
```

---

var   **HTML 4.01 | HTML5**

`<var> . . . </var>`

Indicates an instance of a variable or program argument.

Start/End Tags

Required/Required

Attributes

Core, Internationalization, Events, HTML5 Global Attributes

Example

```
<code><var>myString</var> = 'hello world';</code>
```

video

`<video> . . . </video>`

Embeds a video file in the web page without requiring a plug-in. Authors can provide content in the video element that will be displayed by agents that don't support the **video** element.

Notes

HTML5 only. As of this writing, there is still debate regarding the supported codec for the **video** element (mainly open source Ogg Theora versus the proprietary, yet more popular and more efficient, H.264). **video** is currently supported by Firefox 3.5+, Safari 3.2+, and Opera 10.0+. Chrome support is upcoming. Internet Explorer has not published plans to support **video**.

Start/End Tags

Required/Required

Attributes

HTML5 Global Attributes

`autobuffer` *(autobuffer="autobuffer" in XHTML5)*
    Tells the user agent (browser) that the media file is likely to be used and should be readily available

`autoplay` *(autoplay="autoplay" in XHTML5)*
    Plays the media file automatically

`controls` *(controls="controls" in XHTML5)*
    Indicates that the user agent (browser) should display a set of playback controls for the media file

`height="number"`
    Specifies the height of the video player in pixels

`loop` (loop="loop" *in XHTML5*)
> Indicates that the media file should start playing again from the beginning once it reaches the end

`poster="URL"`
> Specifies the location of a graphic file that displays as a placeholder before the video begins to play

`src="URL"`
> Specifies the location of the media file

`width="number"`
> Specifies the width of the video player in pixels

Examples

See also source listing.

```
<video src="movies/nantucket.ogv" width="640" height="480"
  poster="bay.jpg" type="video/ogg; codecs='theora,
  vorbis'">
  This browser does not support the <code>video</code>
  element.
</video>
```

Elements Organized by Function

This section organizes the elements in HTML 4.01/XHTML 1.0 and HTML5 into groups related to concept or function. Elements that appear in the HTML 4.01 specification only are indicated with (4.01). Elements that appear in HTML5 only are indicated with (5).

Structural elements

body, head, html, meta, title

Semantic text elements

abbr, acronym (4.01), address, article (5), aside (5), blockquote, cite, code, del, dfn, div, em, figure (5), footer (5), h1–h6, header (5), hgroup (5), ins, kbd, mark (5), nav (5), p, pre, q, samp, section (5), small (5), span, strong, sub, sup, var

Presentational text elements

b, basefont (4.01), big (4.01), font (4.01), i, s (4.01), small (4.01), strike (4.01), tt (4.01), u (4.01)

Other text formatting elements

bdo, br, center (4.01), hr

Lists

dd, dir (4.01), dl, dt, li, menu, ol, ul

Tables

caption, col, colgroup, table, tbody, td, tfoot, th, thead, tr

Links

a, base, link

Embedded content

applet (4.01), area, audio (5), embed (5), iframe, img, map, object, param, source (5), video (5)

Frames

frame (4.01), frameset (4.01), noframe (4.01)

Forms

button, datalist (5), fieldset, form, input, isindex (4.01), keygen (5), label, legend, optgroup, option, output (5), select, textarea

---

Style

`style`

Scripts

`script`, `noscript`

Time and measurement

`meter` (5), `progress` (5), `time` (5)

Ruby annotation

`rp` (5), `rt` (5), `ruby` (5)

Interactive

`canvas` (5), `details` (5), `command` (5)

Character Entities

Characters not found in the normal alphanumeric character set, such as < and &, must be specified in HTML and XHTML documents using character references. This process is known as *escaping* the character. In (X)HTML documents, escaped characters are indicated by character references that begin with & and end with ;. The character may be referred to by its Numeric Character Reference (NCR) or a predefined character entity name.

A Numeric Character Reference refers to a character by its Unicode code point in either decimal or hexadecimal form. Decimal character references use the syntax &#nnnn;. Hexadecimal values are indicated by an "x": &#xhhhh;. For example, the less-than (<) character could be identified as < (decimal) or &#x3C (hexadecimal).

Character entities are abbreviated names for characters, such as < for the less-than symbol. Character entities are predefined in the DTDs of markup languages such as HTML and XHMTL as a convenience to authors because they may be easier to remember than Numeric Character References.

ASCII Character Set

HTML and XHTML documents use the standard 7-bit ASCII character set in their source. The first 31 characters in ASCII (not listed) are such device controls as backspace (&#08;) and carriage return () and are not appropriate for use in HTML documents.

HTML 4.01 defines only four entities in this character range—less than (<,<), greater than (<, >), ampersand (&, &), and quotation mark (", ")—that are necessary for escaping characters that may be interpreted as markup. XHTML also includes the ' entity that is included in every XML language. In XHTML documents, the ampersand symbol (&) must always be escaped in attribute values. For better compatibility with XML parsers, authors should use numerical character references instead of named character references for all other character entities.

Decimal	Entity	Symbol	Description
 			Space
!		!	Exclamation point
"	"	"	Quotation mark
#		#	Octothorpe
$		$	Dollar symbol
%		%	Percent symbol
&	&	&	Ampersand
'	' **(XML/XHTML only)**	'	Apostrophe (single quote)
(		(	Left parenthesis

Decimal	Entity	Symbol	Description
&#041;		)	Right parenthesis
&#042;		*	Asterisk
&#043;		+	Plus sign
&#044;		,	Comma
&#045;		-	Hyphen
&#046;		.	Period
&#047;		/	Slash
0–9		0–9	Digits 0–9
&#058;		:	Colon
&#059;		;	Semicolon
&#060;	&lt;	<	Less than
&#061;		=	Equals sign
&#062;	&gt;	>	Greater than
&#063;		?	Question mark
&#064;		@	Commercial at sign
A–Z		A–Z	Letters A–Z
&#091;		[	Left square bracket
&#092;		\	Backslash
&#093;		]	Right square bracket
&#094;		^	Caret
&#095;		_	Underscore
&#096;		`	Grave accent (no letter)
a–z		a–z	Letters a–z
&#123;		{	Left curly brace
|		|	Vertical bar
&#125;		}	Right curly brace
&#126;		~	Tilde

Nonstandard Entities (‚–Ÿ)

The character references numbered 130 through 159 are not defined in HTML and therefore are invalid characters that should be avoided.

Some nonstandard numerical entities in this range are supported by browsers (such as — for an em dash); however, they all have standard equivalents (listed in the "General Punctuation" section). If you need an em dash, use — or — instead.

Latin-1 (ISO-8859-1)

Decimal	Entity	Symbol	Description
			Nonbreaking space
¡	¡	¡	Inverted exclamation mark
¢	¢	¢	Cent sign
£	£	£	Pound symbol
¤	¤	¤	General currency symbol
¥	¥	¥	Yen symbol
¦	¦	¦	Broken vertical bar
§	§	§	Section sign
¨	¨	¨	Umlaut
©	©	©	Copyright
ª	ª	ª	Feminine ordinal
«	«	«	Left angle quote
¬	¬	¬	Not sign
­	­	-	Soft hyphen
®	®	®	Registered trademark
¯	¯	¯	Macron accent
°	°	°	Degree sign
±	±	±	Plus or minus

Decimal	Entity	Symbol	Description
&#178;	&sup2;	2	Superscript 2
&#179;	&sup3;	3	Superscript 3
&#180;	&acute;	´	Acute accent (no letter)
&#181;	&micro;	µ	Micron (Greek mu)
&#182;	&para;	¶	Paragraph sign
&#183;	&middot;	·	Middle dot
&#184;	&cedil;	¸	Cedilla
&#185;	&sup1;	1	Superscript 1
&#186;	&ordm;	º	Masculine ordinal
&#187;	&raquo;	»	Right angle quote
&#188;	&frac14;	¼	Fraction one-fourth
&#189;	&frac12;	½	Fraction one-half
&#190;	&frac34;	¾	Fraction three-fourths
&#191;	&iquest;	¿	Inverted question mark
&#192;	&Agrave;	À	Capital A, grave accent
&#193;	&Aacute;	Á	Capital A, acute accent
&#194;	&Acirc;	Â	Capital A, circumflex accent
&#195;	&Atilde;	Ã	Capital A, tilde accent
&#196;	&Auml;	Ä	Capital A, umlaut
&#197;	&Aring	Å	Capital A, ring
&#198;	&AElig;	Æ	Capital AE ligature
&#199;	&Ccedil;	Ç	Capital C, cedilla
&#200;	&Egrave	È	Capital E, grave accent
&#201;	&Eacute;	É	Capital E, acute accent
&#202;	&Ecirc;	Ê	Capital E, circumflex accent
&#203;	&Euml;	Ë	Capital E, umlaut
&#204;	&Igrave;	Ì	Capital I, grave accent
&#205;	&Iacute;	Í	Capital I, acute accent

Decimal	Entity	Symbol	Description
&#206;	&Icirc;	Î	Capital I, circumflex accent
&#207;	&Iuml;	Ï	Capital I, umlaut
&#208;	&ETH;	Ð	Capital eth, Icelandic
&#209;	&Ntilde;	Ñ	Capital N, tilde
&#210;	&Ograve;	Ò	Capital O, grave accent
&#211;	&Oacute;	Ó	Capital O, acute accent
&#212;	&Ocirc;	Ô	Capital O, circumflex accent
&#213;	&Otilde;	Õ	Capital O, tilde accent
&#214;	&Ouml;	Ö	Capital O, umlaut
&#215;	&times;	×	Multiplication sign
&#216;	&Oslash;	Ø	Capital O, slash
&#217;	&Ugrave;	Ù	Capital U, grave accent
&#218;	&Uacute;	Ú	Capital U, acute accent
&#219;	&Ucirc;	Û	Capital U, circumflex accent
&#220;	&Uuml;	Ü	Capital U, umlaut
&#221;	&Yacute;	Ý	Capital Y, acute accent
&#222;	&THORN;	Þ	Capital Thorn, Icelandic
&#223;	&szlig;	ß	Small sz ligature, German
&#224;	&agrave;	à	Small a, grave accent
&#225;	&aacute;	á	Small a, acute accent
&#226;	&acirc;	â	Small a, circumflex accent
&#227;	&atilde;	ã	Small a, tilde
&#228;	&auml;	ä	Small a, umlaut
&#229;	&aring;	å	Small a, ring
&#230;	&aelig;	æ	Small ae ligature
&#231;	&ccedil;	ç	Small c, cedilla
&#232;	&egrave;	è	Small e, grave accent
&#233;	&eacute;	é	Small e, acute accent

Decimal	Entity	Symbol	Description
ê	ê	ê	Small e, circumflex accent
ë	ë	ë	Small e, umlaut
ì	ì	ì	Small i, grave accent
í	í	í	Small i, acute accent
î	î	î	Small i, circumflex accent
ï	ï	ï	Small i, umlaut
ð	ð	ð	Small eth, Icelandic
ñ	ñ	ñ	Small n, tilde
ò	ò	ò	Small o, grave accent
ó	ó	ó	Small o, acute accent
ô	ô	ô	Small o, circumflex accent
õ	õ	õ	Small o, tilde
ö	ö	ö	Small o, umlaut
÷	÷	÷	Division sign
ø	ø	ø	Small o, slash
ù	ù	ù	Small u, grave accent
ú	ú	ú	Small u, acute accent
û	û	û	Small u, circumflex accent
ü	ü	ü	Small u, umlaut
ý	ý	ý	Small y, acute accent
þ	þ	þ	Small thorn, Icelandic
ÿ	ÿ	ÿ	Small y, umlaut

Latin Extended-A

Decimal	Entity	Symbol	Description
Œ	Œ	Œ	Capital ligature OE
œ	œ	œ	Small ligature oe
Š	Š	Š	Capital S, caron

Decimal	Entity	Symbol	Description
&#353;	&scaron;	š	Small s, caron
&#376	&Yuml;	Ÿ	Capital Y, umlaut

Latin Extended-B

Decimal	Entity	Symbol	Description
&#402;	&fnof;	ƒ	Small f with hook

Spacing Modifier Letters

Decimal	Entity	Symbol	Description
&#710;	&circ;	ˆ	Circumflex accent
&#732;	&tilde;	˜	Tilde

Greek

Decimal	Entity	Symbol	Description
&#913;	&Alpha;	A	Greek capital alpha
&#914;	&Beta;	B	Greek capital beta
&#915;	&Gamma;	Γ	Greek capital gamma
&#916;	&Delta;	Δ	Greek capital delta
&#917;	&Epsilon;	E	Greek capital epsilon
&#918;	&Zeta;	Z	Greek capital zeta
&#919;	&Eta;	H	Greek capital eta
&#920;	&Theta;	θ	Greek capital theta
&#921;	&Iota;	I	Greek capital iota
&#922;	&Kappa;	K	Greek capital kappa
&#923;	&Lambda;	Λ	Greek capital lambda
&#924;	&Mu;	M	Greek capital mu
&#925;	&Nu;	N	Greek capital nu

Decimal	Entity	Symbol	Description
&#926;	&Xi;	Ξ	Greek capital xi
&#927;	&Omicron;	O	Greek capital omicron
&#928;	&Pi;	Π	Greek capital pi
&#929;	&Rho;	P	Greek capital rho
&#931;	&Sigma;	Σ	Greek capital sigma
&#932;	&Tau;	T	Greek capital tau
&#933;	&Upsilon;	Υ	Greek capital upsilon
&#934;	&Phi;	Φ	Greek capital phi
&#935;	&Chi;	Χ	Greek capital chi
&#936;	&Psi;	Ψ	Greek capital psi
&#937;	&Omega;	Ω	Greek capital omega
&#945;	&alpha;	α	Greek small alpha
&#946;	&beta;	β	Greek small beta
&#947;	&gamma;	γ	Greek small gamma
&#948;	&delta;	δ	Greek small delta
&#949;	&epsilon;	ε	Greek small epsilon
&#950;	&zeta;	ζ	Greek small zeta
&#951;	&eta;	η	Greek small eta
&#952;	&theta;	θ	Greek small theta
&#953;	&iota;	ι	Greek small iota
&#954;	&kappa;	κ	Greek small kappa
&#955;	&lambda;	λ	Greek small lambda
&#956;	&mu;	μ	Greek small mu
&#957;	&nu;	ν	Greek small nu
&#958;	&xi;	ξ	Greek small xi
&#959;	&omicron;	o	Greek small omicron
&#960;	&pi;	π	Greek small pi
&#961;	&rho;	ρ	Greek small rho

Decimal	Entity	Symbol	Description
ς	ς	ς	Greek small letter final sigma
σ	σ	σ	Greek small sigma
τ	τ	τ	Greek small tau
υ	υ	υ	Greek small upsilon
φ	φ	φ	Greek small phi
χ	χ	χ	Greek small chi
ψ	ψ	ψ	Greek small psi
ω	ω	ω	Greek small omega
ϑ	ϑ	ϑ	Greek small theta symbol
ϒ	ϒ	ϒ	Greek upsilon with hook
ϖ	ϖ	ϖ	Greek pi symbol

General Punctuation

Decimal	Entity	Symbol	Description
			En space
			Em space
			Thin space
‌	‌	Nonprinting	Zero-width nonjoiner
‍	‍	Nonprinting	Zero-width joiner
‎	‎	Nonprinting	Left-to-right mark
&#8207	‏	Nonprinting	Right-to-left mark
–	–	-	En dash
—	—	—	Em dash
‘	‘	'	Left single quotation mark
’	’	'	Right single quotation mark
‚	‚	‚	Single low-9 quotation mark
“	“	"	Left double quotation mark
”	”	"	Right double quotation mark

Decimal	Entity	Symbol	Description
&#8222;	&bdquo;	„	Double low-9 quotation mark
&#8224;	&dagger;	†	Dagger
&#8225;	&Dagger;	‡	Double dagger
&#8226;	&bull;	•	Bullet
&#8230;	&hellep;	...	Ellipses
&#8240;	&permil;	‰	Per mille symbol (per thousand)
&#8242;	&prime;	′	Prime, minutes, feet
&#8243;	&Prime;	″	Double prime, seconds, inches
&#8249;	&lsaquo;	‹	Single left angle quotation (nonstandard)
&#8250;	&rsaquo;	›	Single right angle quotation (nonstandard)
&#8254;	&oline;	‾	Overline
&#8260;	&frasl;	/	Fraction slash
&#8364;	&euro;	€	Euro symbol

Letter-like Symbols

Decimal	Entity	Symbol	Description
&#8465;	&image;	ℑ	Blackletter capital I, imaginary part
&#8472;	&weierp;	℘	Script capital P, power set
&#8476;	&real;	ℜ	Blackletter capital R, real part
&#8482;	&trade;	™	Trademark sign
&#8501;	&alefsym;	ℵ	Alef symbol, or first transfinite cardinal

Arrows

Decimal	Entity	Symbol	Description
&#8592;	&larr;	←	Left arrow
&#8593;	&uarr;	↑	Up arrow
&#8594;	&rarr;	→	Right arrow
&#8595;	&darr;	↓	Down arrow
&#8596;	&harr;	↔	Left-right arrow
&#8629;	&crarr;	↵	Down arrow with corner leftward
&#8656;	&lArr;	⇐	Leftward double arrow
&#8657;	&uArr;	⇑	Upward double arrow
&#8658;	&rArr;	⇒	Rightward double arrow
&#8659;	&dArr;	⇓	Downward double arrow
&#8660;	&hArr;	⇔	Left-right double arrow

Mathematical Operators

Decimal	Entity	Symbol	Description
&#8704;	&forall;	∀	For all
&#8706;	&part;	∂	Partial differential
&#8707;	&exist;	∃	There exists
&#8709;	&empty;	∅	Empty set, null set, diameter
&#8711;	&nabla;	∇	Nabla, backward difference
&#8712;	&isin;	∈	Element of
&#8713	&notin;	∉	Not an element of
&#8715;	&ni;	∋	Contains as a member
&#8719;	&prod;	∏	N-ary product, product sign
&#8721;	&sum;	∑	N-ary summation
&#8722;	&minus;	−	Minus sign
&#8727;	&lowast;	∗	Asterisk operator
&#8730;	&radic;	√	Square root, radical sign

Decimal	Entity	Symbol	Description
&#8733;	&prop;	∝	Proportional
&#8734;	&infin;	∞	Infinity symbol
&#8736;	&ang;	∠	Angle
&#8743;	&and;	∧	Logical and, wedge
&#8744;	&or;	∨	Logical or, vee
&#8745;	&cap;	∩	Intersection, cap
&#8746;	&cup;	∪	Union, cup
&#8747;	&int;	∫	Integral
&#8756;	&there4;	∴	Therefore
&#8764;	&sim;	~	Tilde operator, varies with, similar to
&#8773;	&cong;	≅	Approximately equal to
&#8776;	&ap;	≈	Almost equal to, asymptotic to
&#8800;	&ne;	≠	Not equal to
&#8801;	&equiv;	≡	Identical to
&#8804;	&le;	≤	Less than or equal to
&#8805;	&ge;	≥	Greater than or equal to
&#8834;	&sub;	⊂	Subset of
&#8835;	&sup;	⊃	Superset of
&#8836;	&nsub;	⊄	Not a subset of
&#8838;	&sube;	⊆	Subset of or equal to
&#8839;	&supe;	⊇	Superset of or equal to
&#8853;	&oplus;	⊕	Circled plus, direct sum
&#8855;	&otimes;	⊗	Circled times, vector product
&#8869;	&perp;	⊥	Up tack, orthogonal to, perpendicular
&#8901;	&sdot;	·	Dot operator

Miscellaneous Technical Symbols

Decimal	Entity	Symbol	Description
⌈	⌈	⌈	Left ceiling
⌉	⌉	⌉	Right ceiling
⌊	⌊	⌊	Left floor
⌋	&rfloor	⌋	Right floor
〈	⟨	⟨	Left-pointing angle bracket
〉	⟩	⟩	Right-pointing angle bracket

Geometric Shapes

Decimal	Entity	Symbol	Description
◊	◊	◊	Lozenge

Miscellaneous Symbols

Decimal	Entity	Symbol	Description
♠	♠	♠	Black spade suit
♣	&clubs	♣	Black club suit
♥	♥	♥	Black heart suit
♦	&diams	♦	Black diamond suit

Specifying Color

Because color is presentational, it should be specified with Cascading Style Sheets, not HTML attributes. This material is included only for completeness.

In both (X)HTML and CSS, color values may be provided by numeric values or standardized color names.

RGB Values

The most common and precise way to specify a color is by its numeric RGB (red, green, blue) values. Using an image-editing tool such as Adobe Photoshop, you can determine the RGB values (on a scale from 0 to 255) for a selected color. For example:

Red: 212 Green: 232 Blue: 119

These values must be converted to their hexadecimal (base-16) equivalents in order to be used as attribute values. In this example, the previous decimal values are converted to hexadecimal:

Red: D4 Green: E8 Blue: 77

In (X)HTML, these values are provided in a six-character string, preceded by the # symbol, like so:

`#D4E877`

The underlying syntax is this:

`#RRGGBB`

where `RR` stands for the hexadecimal red value, `GG` stands for the hexadecimal green value, and `BB` stands for the hexadecimal blue value.

Fortunately, Adobe Photoshop makes the hexadecimal values for colors readily available at the bottom of the color picker next to the # symbol. The hex values can be copied from the color picker and pasted into a style sheet or HTML document.

If you are using an image tool that does not list hexadecimal values, you'll need to convert decimal to hexadecimal yourself using a hexadecimal calculator. Windows users can find a hexadecimal calculator in the "Scientific" view of the Windows standard calculator. On the Mac, the standard calculator has a "Programmer" view (from the menu, select View→Programmer) that can convert decimal to hexadecimal.

Standard Color Names

Colors may also be identified by predefined color names. The syntax for using color names is extremely straightforward:

```
<body link="navy">
```

HTML 4.01 and XHTML 1.0 include 16 valid color names. They are listed here with their equivalent RGB values:

black	#000000	green	#008000
silver	#C0C0C0	lime	#00FF00
gray	#808080	olive	#808000
white	#FFFFFF	yellow	#FFFF00
maroon	#800000	navy	#000080
red	#FF0000	blue	#0000FF
purple	#800080	teal	#008080
fuchsia	#FF00FF	aqua	#00FFFF

These color names may be used with style sheets as well. The CSS 2.1 Recommendation adds orange (#FFA500) to this list for a total of 17 supported colors. CSS 3 supports 140 additional standard color names that are widely supported by browsers, but they are not valid for use in (X)HTML documents.

Index

We'd like to hear your suggestions for improving our indexes. Send email to *index@oreilly.com*.

Get even more for your money.